Trade and Privateer
173:

Fire Ant Books

Trade and Privateering in Spanish Florida, 1732–1763

JOYCE ELIZABETH HARMAN

With a New Introduction by Carl E. Swanson

THE UNIVERSITY OF ALABAMA PRESS

Tuscaloosa

Library of Congress Cataloging-in-Publication Data

Harman, Joyce Elizabeth.
Trade and privateering in Spanish Florida, 1732–1763 / Joyce Elizabeth
Harman ; introduction to the 2004 edition, Carl E. Swanson.
p. cm.
Originally published: St. Augustine Historical Society, 1969.
Includes bibliographical references and index.
ISBN 0-8173-5120-5 (pbk. : alk. paper)
1. Florida—Commerce—History—18th century. 2. Privateering—Florida—
History—18th century. I. Title. HF3161.F7H34 2004
382'.09759'0171241—dc22
2003025371

History is a near-sacred thing, for it must be true and where the truth is, there is God.

Miguel de Cervantes Saavedra

CONTENTS

PREFACE

When we cast an eye on the vast tract of land, and immense riches which the Spanish nation have acquired in America, insomuch that the simple privilege of trading with them, on very high terms, is become a prize worth contending for among the greatest powers in Europe; surely we must acknowledge, that the preservation and enlargement of the British settlements in those parts, will be of the utmost consequence to the trade, interest, and strength of Great Britain.[1]

—South-Carolina Gazette (1763)

The Spanish Empire was, indeed, vast and Great Britain's steady infringement on the trade and territory of Spain in the New World was perhaps the basic cause of inevitable conflicts and disputes with Spain in regard to America.

After the discovery of the New World in 1492 a struggle ensued among the maritime powers in Europe over the rights to trade and to acquire territory there. Spain and Portugal hoped to exclude all other nations from the new lands but were unable to do so. After 1555 Great Britain claimed the right to visit those parts of the Indies not actually held by Spain. The English interpreted ambiguous articles in the treaties of 1604 and 1630 as admitting Englishmen to the Indies and the Spaniards as excluding them.

In the Treaty of Münster in 1648 with the Dutch, the Spanish crown first acknowledged the right of another nation to trade and acquire territory in the East and West Indies.[2] Nineteen years later (1667) Spain first acknowledged the right of the British to their trade and territory in America,[3] but this did not end the contention and competition between them either in the West Indies or on the mainland.

By the eighteenth century Great Britain had a firm grip on the Atlantic seaboard and held Jamaica in the West Indies. From these colonies British subjects engaged in a profitable traffic with the Spanish-American colonies throughout the Empire in violation of the strict Spanish trade laws. In the Southeast the Georgia dispute further complicated the relationship between the Spaniards and the English by heightening tension and suspicion on both sides. In this study I hope to show that the illicit trade between the English—especially in South Carolina, Georgia, and New York—and the Spaniards at Saint Augustine not only existed but benefited both the Spanish and English colonists. When the trade halted as in time of war both suffered, especially the Spaniards. Spanish Florida early in the eighteenth century—perhaps earlier— turned toward the English colonies for supplies. The Florida garrison welcomed and needed the English goods because the colony did not receive adequate supplies from Spanish sources. Yet Spanish Florida in the eighteenth century was not the totally helpless frontier outpost so often pictured. In exchange for the much-needed English goods the Spanish colony sent back to her English neighbors not only gold and silver but also the produce of her own soil. Oranges grown in Spanish Florida appeared at tables in Charleston, Philadelphia, and New York. Here in the Spanish Southeast, a regular trade grew up between Florida and her English neighbors in spite of the bitter intercolonial and international rivalries of the eighteenth century.

I undertook this study upon the suggestion and under the able direction of Professor John Jay TePaske then at The Ohio State University and currently at Duke University. For his enthusiastic, inspiring, and generous guidance, for his many kindnesses, and for the introduction to that most exciting search or quest of all —the search for truth—I am most deeply appreciative. I only hope that this study will in some small way add to that search. Any errors, however, in fact or interpretation are mine alone.

I am indebted also to other individuals and institutions. Miss Mary H. Flower, of London, England, spent many hours at the Public Record Office searching for the manifests of cargoes.

Mr. Terry Campbell of The Ohio State University drew all of the maps, and Mrs. Carol Scherer typed the manuscript. I am most grateful, of course, to the staff at the Saint Augustine Historical Society for their interest in publishing this study.

Finally, I owe a special debt of gratitude to my parents, and also to my sister, Susan—who went over the entire manuscript. Last—but by no means least—I am especially indebted to Mia.

Columbus, Ohio   Joyce Elizabeth Harman

FOOTNOTES

PREFACE

1. *South-Carolina Gazette* (Charleston), May 7-14, 1763. (Hereafter cited as *Gazette.*)
2. Frances Gardiner Davenport, ed., *European Treaties Bearing on the History of the United States and Its Dependencies*, I (Washington, D.C., 1917), 1, 5-7.
3. *Ibid.*, p. 99.

INTRODUCTION TO THE 2004 EDITION
Carl E. Swanson

During the eighteenth century British colonists in South Carolina viewed St. Augustine, Florida, with mixed emotions. On the positive side, the Spanish port was the scene of a thriving, but illegal, trade in which British colonial merchants profited from supplying foodstuffs to the Spaniards. This commerce was crucial for St. Augustine's survival. Charleston businessman Robert Pringle emphasized Florida's dependence: "The Spainards in Augustine would Starve if they were not Supply'd with provissions &c. from our own Plantations. . . ."[1] On the other hand, Charleston merchants and lowcountry planters constantly feared and criticized their southern neighbors. Carolinians claimed that St. Augustine warships illegally seized British vessels in peacetime.[2] During the century's lengthy imperial wars, St. Augustine's privateers captured numerous merchantmen bound to and from Charleston.[3] South Carolinians also asserted that St. Augustine intrigued with powerful southeastern Indian tribes to keep the frontier in constant turmoil.[4] Lowcountry slaveholders believed St. Augustine officials encouraged slave unrest in the Palmetto Colony and were partially responsible for the deadly Stono slave rebellion in 1739.[5] In fact, it is hard to find a Carolina colonist who said anything positive about St. Augustine until the conclusion of the French and Indian War. In 1763, Henry Laurens, another Charleston merchant, was thrilled to learn that St. Augustine was about to become a British possession: "The accession of Florida . . . will prove an excellent barrier to us & open a boundless field for new Trade as well as prove a horrible Check to the Spaniards."[6]

The fears that plagued colonial South Carolinians form the major themes of Joyce Elizabeth Harman's *Trade and Privateering in Spanish Florida, 1732–1763*. Published more than thirty years ago, Harman's book remains one of the most important studies of the First Spanish Period (1565–1763) of Florida's history.[7] St. Augustine occupied the northernmost frontier position in Spain's New World empire. Situated on land of dubious economic value, the settlement nonetheless played an important role in Spanish America. It prevented southern expansion by the British colonies of South Carolina and Georgia and checked eastward development of the French colony of Mississippi. In addition, St. Augustine stood athwart the homeward-bound course of the Spanish treasure fleets.

Although St. Augustine played an important military role in Spanish imperialism, it largely failed to live up to the expectations assigned to colonies by advocates of mercantilism, the era's dominant economic theory. Spain's eighteenth-century imperial administrators wanted to keep colonial commerce within the empire; colonies were expected to export commodities to Spain or other Spanish colonies and purchase manufactured goods from the mother country in return. The *flotas* and *galeones* brought European goods from Spain to Mexico, Peru, and the other Spanish colonies. Havana, Cuba, served as the rendezvous port and Caribbean shipping center for the treasure fleets that carried home the colonies' silver and gold. This closed economic system worked fairly well for the empire's most valuable possessions. The system did not work for St. Augustine, however.

St. Augustine's efforts to evade Spain's mercantilist imperial system and engage in illicit trade with Britain's North American colonies constitute the book's major argument. When imperial warfare largely prevented commerce with British North America, St. Augustinians turned to privateering. Obviously, Spanish officials frowned on the colony's commercial relations outside the empire. Similarly, Robert Pringle's comments reveal that many British officials and merchants held antagonistic views of St. Augustine. Yet illegal commerce could be mutually beneficial for many Spanish and British colonists, and forbidden trade characterizes St. Augustine's experience in the eighteenth century.

Harman traces in detail how the Florida outpost never developed a self-sustaining commercial economy. Instead, St. Augustine depended on an inadequate government subsidy, the *situado*. Consequently, Florida officials and merchants were forced to ignore the mercantilist restrictions prohibiting trade with foreign nationals and engaged in commerce with Britain's North American colonies. South Carolina and Georgia were St. Augustine's most important British trading partners, but New York and New England merchants also dispatched vessels to Florida. St. Augustine constantly needed foodstuffs to feed its important military garrison as well as its civilian population. Because of inadequate supplies from Spain, British manufactured goods were always in demand. In exchange for provisions, Florida traders sold cargoes of oranges and fish. The oranges were especially popular in Charleston. In fact, during the 1740s merchants in the South Carolina capital tried to establish their own export trade in oranges. Robert Pringle and Henry Laurens sent numerous chests of oranges to customers in London, Boston, New York, Philadelphia, and Virginia. The South Carolina orange exporting business was short-lived, however. Unusually cold weather in early 1748 wiped out virtually all of South Carolina's orange trees.[8] Florida orange growers were still in business. The illicit commerce between St. Augustine and the British provinces was mutually beneficial, and local officials largely ignored imperial directives to end this traffic.

Harman demonstrates that the eighteenth century's intercolonial wars accomplished what royal *cédulas* could not. During the War of Jenkins's Ear and King George's War (1739–48) and the French and Indian War (1755–63) commerce between St. Augustine and British North America ground to halt. Privateering became the most important economic enterprise in St. Augustine and throughout America generally. Hundreds of private warships plied New World shipping lanes in search of valuable prizes. St. Augustine played a leading role in Spanish privateering ventures during the 1740s. In fact, the Florida outpost ranked second only to Havana as the most important privateering port in the Spanish Empire.[9] With support from Governor Manuel de Montiano, who personally invested in privateering ventures, numerous Florida privateers attacked Britain's most valuable North American commerce. Spanish captains captured British vessels off the Carolina coast and the Virginia and Delaware capes. In 1744, Spanish privateers often sailed in consort with French commerce raiders when France joined the war against Great Britain. Only the peace treaty of Aix-la-Chapelle in 1748 stopped successful privateering voyages.

Harman emphasizes that St. Augustine's privateering enterprise was motivated by more than patriotism and windfall profits. The colony's economy had depended heavily on trade with British North America. When hostilities closed that avenue of commerce, St. Augustine's merchants and mariners turned to privateering for their economic survival. Governor Montiano stressed the colony's dire straits with imperial officials. St. Augustine's predators needed to capture British vessels carrying rice, wheat, and other foodstuffs or the colony would starve.

As soon as war ended in 1748, trade resumed between St. Augustine and its northern neighbors. In fact, Harman shows that British colonists connived to trade in St. Augustine *during* the wars of 1739–48 as well as in the subsequent French and Indian War. British vessels entered St. Augustine under "flags of truce." The captains of these vessels had obtained permits to exchange prisoners of war. Since many flag-of-truce vessels were loaded to the gunwales with valuable commodities but carried only one or two prisoners, the real, commercial purposes of these voyages were clear. Before Spain entered the French and Indian War, a lively trade with British colonists was carried on at St. Augustine despite the fact that many cargoes from this traffic supplied French privateers that fitted out in the Florida capital. When Spain and Britain finally went to war in January 1762, British North American officials implemented stringent measures to end the illicit trade with St. Augustine. In response, Floridians again turned to privateering.

St. Augustine never fit very well in Spain's mercantilist empire. It was a neglected, unpopular outpost on the fringe of Spanish America. Harman argues persuasively that the Florida capital would have faced a desperate existence without the clandestine trade with British North America or the prizes that Spanish privateers captured during the imperial wars that halted peaceful commerce. Ironically, she concludes, "the English colonies, willingly or unwillingly, helped their Spanish neighbor to hold out in the Southeast" (p. 82).

Although *Trade and Privateering in Spanish Florida* appeared more than thirty years ago, this new edition is welcome. Harman focused on three important but neglected issues concerning eighteenth-century America. She wrote about St. Augustine. The Spaniards surely neglected this northern colonial outpost during the 1500s–1800s, and subsequent historians have as well. Harman wrote as well about the interactions of Spanish and British colonies, thus anticipating the popularity of "Atlantic" and "transnational" history as opposed to studies concentrating on individual colonies or empires. Finally, she took privateering seriously and realized that it played a key role in maritime conflict during the age of sail.

Florida is the neglected stepchild of Spain's American empire. Historians have produced few studies of this frontier colony. This is especially true for the First Spanish Period of 1565–1763. *Books about Early America: 2001 Titles*, a leading bibliography of monographs in English, for example, lists only four titles. Of these, only one is devoted to the eighteenth century; two focus on the sixteenth century, while the other covers the period 1565–1702.[10] Historians have begun to pay more attention to early Florida history, but many newer studies focus on the British Period (1763–84) or the Second Spanish Period (1784–1821).

This recent work largely corroborates Harman's view concerning Florida's weak economy. Bernard Bailyn has examined the failure of New Smyrna Plantation, which operated on Florida's central coast from 1768 to 1777.[11] Similarly, David Hancock has discussed Mount Oswald, the unsuccessful plantation in which wealthy British merchant Richard Oswald lost substantial sums.[12] Jane G. Landers has edited a useful collection of essays that examines various aspects of Florida's economic development during both the British Period and the Second Spanish Period.[13] Although some authors disagree with Bailyn's and Hancock's characterizations, these essays emphasize the numerous problems that plagued Florida's colonial economy. These scholars echo Harman's most important arguments. Florida was a frontier colony with a weak economy, and imperial warfare seriously disrupted economic development. The colony desperately depended on trade with its northern neighbors. Eventually, Spanish officials agreed with their colonists that only free trade with the United States would ensure Florida's economic survival. As James Gregory Cusick succinctly puts it: "Cuba sent Spain revenues from its commerce with the United States. Florida sent only bills. Under these circumstances, Spanish interest in the province waned, and Florida's commercial integration with U.S. ports foreshadowed its ultimate political and social absorption into the United States."[14]

Harman focused extensively on St. Augustine's commerce with British provinces, especially South Carolina, demonstrating clearly that Spanish and British colonists interacted regularly. Despite the views of Spain's mercantilist officials and the exclusionary policies formulated in Seville (and London), St. Augustine and Charleston merchants sought one another's business. When imperial warfare interrupted this mutually beneficial illicit trade, St. Augustine businessmen and government officials invested in privateering ventures, because British cargoes were essential for the colony's survival. Thus, thirty years before it became fashionable, Harman was writing what historians have recently termed "Atlantic" or "transnational" history. Harman's work adheres to Nicholas Canny's definition of this "new" history: "Atlantic history certainly calls for comparative investigations across colonies and for the study of problems that were common to more than one settlement...."[15] Harman did not study Spanish Florida in a vacuum; she placed it in its Atlantic context. If she were writing today, she would probably broaden this transnational emphasis by discussing St. Augustine's important role in the diplomatic maneuvering concerning Spain, Great Britain, France, and the Native Americans who were all jockeying for power in the Southeast. She might also have included some thoughts about Florida's interactions with the European powers' Caribbean colonies.

Harman also appreciated the importance of privateering in imperial warfare, which was rare in 1969. Following, perhaps, in the wake of naval and military historians who had denigrated the value of private men of war, most historians of eighteenth-century America largely ignored privateering.[16] Some economic historians even erroneously claimed that privateering declined and was eliminated during the eighteenth century.[17] Harman's work clearly revealed that St. Augustine relied heavily on its privateers during the War of Jenkins's Ear and the French and Indian War. The same was true for British and French America. Many subsequent historians have echoed Harman's emphasis on privateering's importance, and numerous studies of privateering during the eighteenth and early nineteenth centuries appeared after her book.[18] Naval historians have even begun to take privateering and prize actions much more seriously than their predecessors.[19]

Trade and Privateering in Spanish Florida, 1732–1763 has long been out of print. Historians of Spanish and British America will be pleased that Harman's work is available again.

Notes

1. Robert Pringle to John Richards, 27 December 1738, in *The Letterbook of Robert Pringle* (Columbia, S.C.: University of South Carolina Press, 1972), 1:51.

2. See, for example, South Carolina Council to the Board of Trade, 29 September 1720, Records in the British Public Record Office Relating to South Carolina, 7:208; *Pennsylvania Gazette* (Philadelphia), 7 October 1731; *South-Carolina Gazette* (Charleston), 4 June 1741, 25 September 1762.

3. Henry Laurens to James Crokatt, 24 June 1747; Laurens to Crokatt, 18 August 1747; Laurens to Alexander Watson, 7 November 1747; Laurens to Thomas Savage, 18 August 1747, in *The Papers of Henry Laurens* (Columbia, S.C.: University of South Carolina Press, 1968), 1:11, 43, 73, 82–83. The *South-Carolina Gazette* printed thousands of stories about privateering and prizes during the Anglo-Spanish-French wars of 1739–63.

4. See, for example, Joseph Boone and Richard Berresford to the Board of Trade, 5 December 1716; Robert Johnson to the Board of Trade, 12 January 1719; Arthur Middleton to Duke of Newcastle, 13 June 1728; Thomas Broughton to the Board of Trade, October 1735, Records in the British Public Record Office Relating to South Carolina, 6:261; 7:237–44; 13:61–70; 17:396–403.

5. Robert Pringle to Andrew Pringle, 27 December 1739, in *Pringle Letterbook*, 1:163.

6. Laurens to John Knight, 14 February 1763, in *Laurens Papers*, 3:253.

7. Harman's Ohio State University M.A. thesis supervisor, John Jay TePaske, wrote the leading work for this era. See *The Governorship of Spanish Florida, 1700–1763* (Durham, N.C.: Duke University Press, 1964).

8. R. Pringle to A. Pringle, 1 October 1744; R. Pringle to Alexander McKensey, 13 December 1744, in *Pringle Letterbook*, 2:742, 778. Laurens to Alexander Watson, 21 November 1747; Laurens to Thomas Richards, 23 November 1747; Laurens to Thomas Savage, 4 March 1748; Laurens to Ebenezer Holmes, 11 August 1748, in *Laurens Papers*, 1:84, 85, 116, 117. Harman notes on p. 24 that South Carolina exported 418 barrels of oranges as late as 1759, but this was just a drop in the bucket compared to earlier exports.

9. Carl E. Swanson, *Predators and Prizes: American Privateering and Imperial Warfare, 1739–1748* (Columbia, S.C.: University of South Carolina Press, 1991), 145.

10. David L. Ammerman and Philip D. Morgan, comps., *Books about Early America: 2001 Titles* (Williamsburg, Va.: Institute of Early American History and Culture, 1989), 25–27. Interestingly, Ammerman and Morgan failed to list Harman's book, which is another indication of how much this subject has been neglected.

11. Bernard Bailyn, *Voyagers to the West: A Passage in the Peopling of America on the Eve of the Revolution* (New York: Knopf, 1986), 451–61.

12. David Hancock, *Citizens of the World: London Merchants and the Integration of the British Atlantic Community, 1735–1785* (Cambridge: Cambridge University Press, 1995), 153–71.

13. Jane G. Landers, ed., *Colonial Plantations and Economy in Florida* (Gainesville, Fla.: University Press of Florida, 2000).

14. James Gregory Cusick, "Spanish East Florida in the Atlantic Economy of the Late Eighteenth Century," in Landers, *Colonial Plantations*, 184.

15. Nicholas Canny, "Writing Atlantic History; or, Reconfiguring the History of Colonial British America," *Journal of American History* 86 (December 1999): 1108. This article appeared in a special issue of the *JAH* titled "The Nation and Beyond: Transnational Perspectives on United States History." For the continuing popularity of "Atlantic" history among historians of the seventeenth and eighteenth centuries, see Joyce E. Chaplin, "Expansion and Exceptionalism in Early American History," *Journal of American History* 89 (March 2003): 1431–55.

16. See, for example, Alfred Thayer Mahan, *The Influence of Sea Power upon History, 1660–1783* (Boston: Little Brown, 1890); H. W. Richmond, *The Navy in the War of 1739–48*, 3 vols. (Cambridge: Cambridge University Press, 1920); Douglas Edward Leach, *Arms for Empire: A Military History of the British Colonies in North America, 1607–1763* (New York: Macmillan, 1973).

17. Douglass C. North, "Sources of Productivity Change in Ocean Shipping, 1600–1850," *Journal of Political Economy* 76 (1968): 953–70; James F. Shepherd and Gary M. Walton, *Shipping, Maritime Trade, and the Economic Development of Colonial North America* (Cambridge: Cambridge University Press, 1972).

18. Jerome R. Garitee, *The Republic's Private Navy: The American Privateering Business as Practiced by Baltimore during the War of 1812* (Middletown, Conn.: Wesleyan University Press and Mystic Seaport, 1977); Patrick Crowhurst, *The French War on Trade: Privateering 1793–1815* (Aldershot, England: Scolar Press, 1989); David J. Starkey, *British Privateering Enterprise in the Eighteenth Century* (Exeter, England: Fern Canyon Press, 1990); Swanson, *Predators and Prizes*; Faye Margaret Kert, *Prize and Prejudice: Privateering and Naval Prize in Atlantic Canada in the War of 1812* (St. John's, Newfoundland, Canada: International Maritime Economic History Association, 1997).

19. Julian Gwyn, *The Enterprising Admiral: The Personal Fortune of Admiral Sir Peter Warren* (Montreal: McGill-Queen's University Press, 1974); Richard Harding, *Seapower and Naval Warfare, 1650–1830* (Annapolis, Md.: Naval Institute Press, 1999).

Trade and Privateering in Spanish Florida, 1732–1763

CHAPTER I

INTRODUCTION

In the latter half of the eighteenth century Great Britain won the contest for supremacy in North America by defeating France and Spain in the French and Indian War. For nearly two hundred years the three nations had engaged in a struggle for colonial dominance. This struggle resulted in four inter-colonial wars, the first beginning in 1689 and the last ending in 1763, separated only by periods of uneasy peace.

The Southeast was significant in intercolonial and international rivalries. Here the chief contestants were Spain and Great Britain. Spain claimed (until 1763) the region south and west of Charleston, but the English, pushing ever southward, established Georgia in 1733 to challenge this claim. The diplomatic dispute over the territory and the struggle for supremacy which developed in this part of North America occupied the diplomats of both nations, and upon occasion their military forces, especially during the early part of the eighteenth century.[1]

The dispute over navigation in the West Indies was a major factor too in intercolonial and international disputes. The merchants of Great Britain habitually violated the strict Spanish trade regulations and treaties with Spain and then complained vigorously about the reprisals they incurred at the hands of the Spanish officials. Persisting in their illicit trade in Spanish-American waters, they petitioned the British government for redress of their grievances. In 1739 this pressure was so great that Prime Minister Robert Walpole, who favored peace, had to give in, and the War of Jenkins' Ear ensued. This war, as was the case in previous and succeeding intercolonial wars, acted not only as a stimulant to privateering but to illicit commerce as well.

The relationship in the Southeast between the English colonies of North Carolina, South Carolina and Georgia, and Spanish

Florida during the period 1732-1763 must be considered in light of intercolonial disputes and rivalries. The Spaniards at Saint Augustine lived in fear of the English from the middle of the seventeenth century,[2] and the Englishmen likewise feared the Spaniards, yet the illicit commerce went on. A flourishing trade grew up between Charleston and Saint Augustine, despite the fact that Spanish laws forbade trade with foreign colonies. These restrictions were often ignored, however, especially when the Saint Augustine garrison was in desperate need of supplies.[3]

Even though she was far removed from the major centers of Spanish colonial civilization,[4] Spanish Florida was important to Spain. Saint Augustine was well located for the protection of the colonial trade and commerce of Spain, though not so well located as a site for a colony.[5] Spain, therefore, maintained Florida chiefly for the protection and relief of her colonial commerce and as a defensive frontier in the north.[6] Because of the difficulty in maintaining an adequate flow of supplies to Saint Augustine from Spain or her nearby colonies, the garrison was frequently in desperate straits and the settlers and soldiers prior to the eighteenth century often faced poverty and starvation.[7] Thus the Spaniards in Saint Augustine often found it necessary to ignore the strict royal trade restrictions and to import supplies from the nearby English colonies.[8]

FOOTNOTES

CHAPTER I

INTRODUCTION

1. John Tate Lanning, *The Diplomatic History of Georgia: A Study of the Epoch of Jenkins' Ear* (Chapel Hill, 1936), p. vii. (Hereafter cited as Lanning, *Diplomatic History of Georgia*.)

2. Verne E. Chatelain, *The Defenses of Spanish Florida, 1565 to 1763* (Washington, D.C., 1941), p. 32. (Hereafter cited as Chatelain, *Defenses of Spanish Florida*.)

3. *Ibid.*, pp. 21-22; John Jay TePaske, *The Governorship of Spanish Florida, 1700-1763* (Durham, 1964), pp. 71, 88-89, 105, (hereafter cited as TePaske, *Governorship of Spanish Florida*); Library of Congress, East

The Town & Harbour of Saint Augustine, 1733

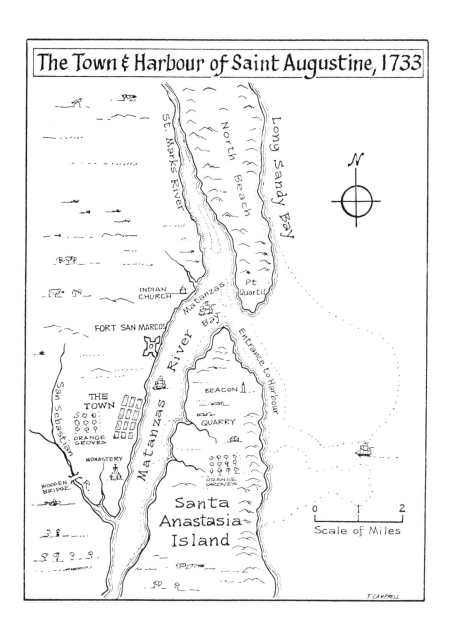

St. Marks River

North Beach

Long Sandy Bay

N

INDIAN CHURCH

Matanzas

Pt. Quartil

FORT SAN MARCOS

Matanzas River Bay

Entrance to Harbour

San Sebastian

THE TOWN

BEACON

QUARRY

ORANGE GROVES

MONASTERY

WOODEN BRIDGE

ORANGE GROVES

Santa Anastasia Island

0   1   2
Scale of Miles

T. CAMPBELL

Florida Papers, Letters to the Captain General (Montiano Letters), March 22, 1737 - January 31, 1741, L.C. 37, copies, (hereafter cited as Montiano Letters).

4. Herbert E. Bolton, *The Spanish Borderlands, A Chronicle of Old Florida and the Southwest* (New Haven, 1921), p. vii. (Hereafter cited as Bolton, *Spanish Borderlands*.)

5. Chatelain, *Defenses of Spanish Florida*, p. 14.

6. *Ibid.*, p. 21.

7. *Ibid.*, p. 22.

8. TePaske, *Governorship of Spanish Florida*, p. 163.

CHAPTER II
TRADE AND THE DEVELOPMENT OF AN
ORANGE INDUSTRY IN FLORIDA,
1717-1739

During the greater part of the eighteenth century, mercantilism was still the prevailing economic policy in Europe. In theory, mercantilism stressed the importance of maintaining a favorable balance of trade by increasing exports and decreasing imports, thus accumulating gold and silver which was then believed to be the real basis of wealth. Both the Spanish and English colonial commercial systems were based on this theory and were, therefore, protectionist—both believed that their colonies existed primarily for the benefit of the mother country. In America, however, the trade restrictions of both Spain and Great Britain were quite commonly ignored by both the Spaniards and the English and illicit trade flourished. Spain, especially, attempted to prevent and halt the illicit trade with her colonies, but without much success as the trade was highly profitable for the English and often welcomed by the colonial Spaniards.

The Spanish Restrictions

The Spanish-American Empire until late in the eighteenth century was subject to stringent trade restrictions. Spain's colonial system, based on the mercantilist philosophy, was extremely monopolistic, the purpose of the Spanish crown being to create for Spain a monopoly of all trade and shipping with her colonies, but without much success as the trade was highly silver which the colonies produced in such vast amounts. The Spanish laws, therefore, excluded all foreigners from trading directly with the Spanish-American ports and reserved the external trade of the colonies exclusively to Spain. The law required that all goods be shipped to the colonies from Spain on Spanish vessels, and forbade the export of gold and silver to

4

foreign countries. All these restrictions, nevertheless, were oftentimes ignored and frequently with the connivance of Spanish officials.

The wealth of the vast Spanish Empire proved to be an irresistible temptation to foreign interlopers. Great Britain, for example, allowed her subjects to engage in illicit traffic with the Spanish colonies without interference,[1] (except in time of war) for this brought large quantities of the precious gold and silver into the Kingdom. The Spanish colonists, on the other hand, usually welcomed the British goods which were, of course, cheaper and often of better quality. Buenos Aires was a favorite port for foreign interlopers for over two hundred years, especially since it was far removed from the sources of Spanish control. Jamaica in the West Indies was a center of contraband commerce with her Spanish neighbors, and in the eighteenth century New York and other North American ports enjoyed a profitable trade with Cuba, Puerto Rico, and Española. In the Southeast, Saint Augustine received supplies from New York, South Carolina, and Georgia until 1762 in exchange for gold and silver and/or her colonial produce. Thus, despite the dismay of the Spanish crown, foreign interlopers carried on a flourishing though illicit traffic with Spanish-American ports throughout the Empire.

The Anglo-Spanish Dispute

The Anglo-Spanish dispute with regard to America revolved around the free navigation-contraband trade controversy and the conflicting claims to Georgia. The former controversy grew out of the British violation of both the stringent Spanish trade laws and the treaties between the two crowns.

In a treaty concluded in July, 1670, Great Britain obtained the promise of "kind entertainment" for British vessels in distress in Spanish-American ports and permission to provision and undergo repairs there. This was a concession never before granted by the Spanish crown to any power in any treaty. As the Spaniards feared, however, the English could always pretend to be in distress or to need provisions, and once in a Spanish-American port, an English ship could take advantage of

5

its opportunities. The British later on frequently employed this pretense despite the fact that in 1670 they had not even asked for the liberty to trade in Spanish America. This was in part because the British Navigation Acts were not consistent with reciprocal free trade in that area, and, in part, because the English merchants felt that it was more profitable to ship goods there by way of Spain.[2]

The Treaty of Utrecht in 1713 granted further privileges to the English. Under terms of this treaty, the British South Sea Company obtained an *asiento* (contract) giving to it the exclusive right for thirty years to import and sell annually in the Spanish-American colonies four thousand or more Negro slaves. An additional provision permitted the company to send one shipload of goods to Portobello (Panamá) each year—the ship not to be over six hundred tons burden.[3] English merchants, however, habitually violated the provisions of this and previous treaties, as well as the Spanish trade restrictions. Jamaica was a base for the South Sea Company and for many of the English interlopers who traded their goods at minor Spanish colonial ports in exchange for gold and silver and/or Spanish colonial products.[4] As a result of these violations, Spain increased the number of her *guardacostas* (coastguard vessels) in American waters and gave them instructions to search for contraband goods and to seize such goods and the vessels carrying them. Spain's assertion of the right to search and seize the vessels of other nations sometimes resulted in the capture of innocent as well as guilty traders by the Spanish *guardacostas*. Great Britain, although demanding the right of free navigation without search in American waters and complaining of Spanish depredations, nevertheless continued the illicit traffic which Spain was so determined to prevent.[5]

American waters thus abounded with captures which were rather disruptive to normal trading activities. Rear Admiral Charles Stewart, the commander of the British Naval Forces in the West Indies, received instructions in 1732 regarding more effective measures for preventing the Spaniards in America from disturbing British navigation on the "Pretence" of guarding their own coasts—accounts being received at the time of nine such Spanish ships fitted out from Cuba, Española, and

Puerto Rico.⁶ Rear Admiral Stewart, in his official position, had dutifully complained the previous fall to the governor of Cuba of the violent and villainous actions of the *guardacostas*. But to the Duke of Newcastle, Secretary of State of the Southern Department, Stewart wrote about illicit traders boasting of killing Spaniards on their own coasts. These so-called merchants, Stewart felt, were no better than peddlers and he knew of one who had formerly been in jail for piracy.⁷

But English traders continued to complain about the treatment they suffered at the hands of the Spaniards in American waters. In 1731, for example, his majesty's sloop the *Spence* took a Spanish *guardacosta* and found on board her a newly murdered Englishman.⁸

The *Alice and Elizabeth* in the early morning of December 9, 1731, was on a voyage from Jamaica to Charleston, when she came upon a large vessel off the Bahama Banks. The captain saw her in the moonlight some distance away, but was unable to distinguish her colors. He finally learned that it was a Spanish vessel, but it was too late. Before he could hide the valuables on board his vessel, the Spanish ship was upon him. The Spaniards demanded that the *Alice and Elizabeth* put out her ship's boat. Subsequently, the mate and four hands rowed out to meet their Spanish captors who treated them to the "usual compliments" of hanging burning matches between their fingers. The British mate, who spoke French, talked with the captain of·the Spanish sloop which was mounted with eight cannon and manned with at least seventy men. The Spanish captain did not seem as uncivil as the rest of his crew. The Spaniards, however, hauled the *Alice and Elizabeth* to a shallow place on the banks, anchored it, and stripped the hold of its cargo. After taking money, sails, rum, sugar, and dry goods of considerable value; they stripped the captain, mate, and men of all their clothes and bedding and then allowed them to proceed on their voyage to Charleston, which the Spaniards promised to visit as soon as the cold weather was over.⁹

In September, 1732, a Spanish sloop commanded by Don Pedro of Puerto Rico captured the sloop *Hannah and Lidia* en route from Jamaica to Boston, off the northern side of Cuba. Don Pedro, about twelve days out from Havana on a voyage for Puerto Rico, "robb'd" the English of all their "Cloaths and Beding," some sails, their best cable and anchor, most of their provisions, some sugar, money, "Plate" (precious metals) and two Negro men; the whole amounting to five hundred pounds Jamaican money. In addition the Spaniards beat and abused the men and passengers.[10] Later the same fall, a Spanish galley captured an English perriauger (a small open boat). The Englishmen attempted little if any resistance, but soon found an opportunity to secure their arms and fell upon the Spaniards. Killing most of them, they recaptured their own vessel and then captured the Spanish galley.[11] Some Spaniards in December, 1732, detained the *Amelia* in her passage to Bristol under pretense of searching for logwood, but as they did not find anything on board to make her prizeworthy, they "wished her a good Voyage and discharged her."[12] Seizures by the Spanish *guardacostas* of British vessels involved in illicit trade with the Spanish-American ports continued mainly because the traffic continued. However, the Spanish practice of search and seizure led to some abuses and an occasional honest trader also had his goods taken.

The English retaliated in return. In the fall of 1732, for example, British men-of-war attacked some Spanish privateers or *guardacostas* and inflicted damages, but it was not immediately known if they had been seized. The report from the West Indies noted that if they were taken, "the Spaniards will not be such bad Christians as to seek Revenge, in an Age so famous for bearing of Injuries."[13] Hostilities in American waters were common and contributed greatly to the war in 1739.

Conflicting claims to Georgia were another cause for the war. Sovereignty in the disputed region, according to the Treaty of Utrecht in 1713 and the Treaty of 1721, was to be decided on the basis of the limits in 1700. It was not clear, however, whether these limits were to be decided on the basis of original discovery, royal grants, or actual occupation. The British tried to maintain their claim on all three bases. For example, they cited alleged discoveries made by John Cabot in 1497 along the American coast. On the other hand, the Spanish claim to Georgia included the establishment of Saint Augustine and the expeditions made by Juan Ponce de León and Hernando de Soto.[14] But the English, under the prodding of James Oglethorpe, pushed into the territory also claimed by Spain. Thus, Georgia in the eighteenth century became an important factor in international and intercolonial diplomacy and a definite threat to peace in Europe[15]—as well as in the Southeast.

The dispute over the southern boundary naturally made relations between the English in South Carolina and Georgia and the Spaniards in Saint Augustine somewhat strained and uneasy. Both sides mistrusted the other and feared an attempt at invasion. Afraid of an impending clash, the English adopted defensive measures against the French and Spanish in America.[16] In November, 1734, for instance, Governor Robert Johnson of South Carolina urged a posture of defense and the repair of fortifications, since Oglethorpe regarded the interests of Carolina and Georgia to be inseparable.[17]

Apprehension grew in 1735 with talk of Great Britain entering the war in Europe against Spain and France and the extension of hostilities to America. Reports that the Spaniards intended to attack Savannah alarmed the Georgians in the spring of 1735—especially since the colony lacked a fort, battery, or shelter.[18] However, the Spanish crown suspended in March, 1735, the expedition being prepared at Havana, because of promising negotiations then impending in Europe to settle the boundary dispute peacefully.[19]

But Spain later in the same year again began to make plans to take by force the territory which she felt to belong to her. In the fall of 1735 John Savy, an Englishman who had lived in South Carolina and Georgia, offered his services to the Spanish crown. Savy, who assumed the name of Don Miguel Wall, proposed to aid the Spaniards in routing the English and destroying all their settlements, thereby reducing Carolina and Georgia to the Treaty of Utrecht limits.[20] Not until the summer of 1736 did the English government receive its first hint of an actual Spanish plot against Georgia. Wall had been sent to Havana early that summer,[21] and the South Sea Company factors there reported on his activities and the plot against Georgia.[22]

Spain spent nearly two years preparing for the attack on Georgia. In November, 1737, however, the crown ordered the

9

expedition to be suspended, in part, because Spain was not in a strong enough position to fight for the disputed territory and, in part, because the minister, Don Joseph Patiño, who originally backed the plot, had died. Also the unreliability of Wall was becoming apparent to the Spaniards.[23] Thus the Spanish plot to invade Georgia was not carried out.

Once knowledge of the plot had leaked out, however, it alarmed the English in the Southeast, especially in South Carolina and Georgia, and they remained in a state of apprehension for several years. In November, 1736, for example, the lieutenant governor of South Carolina spoke to the general assembly of that province on the state of the colony's fortifications and steps necessary

> . . . in order that the Artillery which his Majesty has been pleased out of his Royal Favour and Paternal Care of us his distant Subjects to send here may be mounted, and put us in such a Condition of Defence, as may convince our Foreign Neighbors that we are prepar'd for them at all Events.[24]

When Charleston learned in December, 1736, that a man-of-war with a considerable number of soldiers and warlike stores had been sent to Saint Augustine, it appeared that the fears of South Carolina and Georgia regarding the designs of the Spanish were not without foundation.[25] Then in February, 1737, a report published in the South-Carolina Gazette told of the Spaniards landing at Edisto Island and making two families prisoners. The issue of the following week revealed, however, that it had been an English vessel which in a fog was mistaken for a Spanish vessel—surely an example of the Carolinians' uneasiness during this period.[26]

Consequently, the South Carolina government in February, 1737, took steps to prevent "an Invasion."[27] The general assembly ordered the public treasurer to advance to Captain John Parris the sum of three hundred pounds to scour the coasts of South Carolina and Georgia as far down as Saint Augustine.[28] Subsequently the assembly proposed to send another vessel to the coast of Cuba to obtain information concerning the designs of the Spaniards against South Carolina and Georgia.[29] The Georgia colony also had the protection of the sloop *Hawk* plus two ships of war sent by the crown.[30]

Meanwhile, Gabriel Johnston, the governor of North Carolina, delivered a speech to the general assembly of that colony on March 10, 1737, in which he told of receiving news from the governor of South Carolina about an armament of Spanish ships of war and troops preparing at Havana to go to Saint Augustine and from there to attack the new colony of Georgia and the province of South Carolina. Governor Johnston urged the assembly that "the least you can do" is to make a more effective law for raising the militia.[31]

In June, 1737, letters sent to the English factor in Havana ordered all the English who lived there to leave—excepting the factor.[32] The Spanish crown the same spring, however, ordered the English South Sea Company factors expelled from Havana since these factors had supplied their fellow countrymen with reports of the Spanish plot and preparations against Georgia.[33]

Tension grew in the Southeast—sparked by reports, rumors, and fear of the nearby Spaniards. In April, 1738, the governor of South Carolina received "fresh Advices" that "several Vessels" were at anchor off Saint Augustine, and so took measures "to prevent any Surprise." A British man-of-war accompanied by a well-manned sloop thus departed on a cruise to obtain "more certain" information as to the Spanish designs.

A Captain Prew arrived in Charleston the same month with information on the Spanish designs—after being held prisoner at Havana for six months and five days, without being allowed to speak to anyone except the person who brought his food. Prew said that the Spaniards intended to use him as a pilot in their attack on Georgia that spring, but two days before sailing, new orders came from Spain to stop the expedition. The Spanish then released him and sent him in a man-of-war to Saint Augustine. The captain told of the arrival there at the same time of 2 snows (a square-rigged vessel similar to a brigantine), 2 ships, 1 schooner, and 2 sloops loaded with provisions, ammunition, and 500 recruits. These along with other troops from Havana totaling 7000 men, 37 pinnaces and lances and 6 half-galleys then in the port, were intended for the expedition against Georgia, but for the contra orders.

11

The *South-Carolina Gazette* noted *"If these Orders are true feigned, Time will learn."*[34] For the English were, of course, still apprehensive because they did not yet know that the Spanish crown actually issued the contra order late in 1737,[35] which arrived at Havana barely in time to halt the long-feared invasion.

Meanwhile, Don Miguel Wall, alias John Savy, had talked too freely and aroused the suspicion of the Spaniards. The crown in the spring of 1737 ordered that he be sent back to Spain.[36] After being sent to Spain, Wall managed to elude the Spanish and made his way to London in November, 1737. There he claimed to be the person who had captured most of the English ships taken into Havana by the Spanish *guardacostas*. A British subject, though lately in the service of the king of Spain, he claimed that he had absolute orders from the Spanish king to take all English vessels with or without contraband goods and carry them in. He left the Spanish service "being touched over with Remorse at so unjust a Proceeding," despite his salary of one thousand *pistoles* a year. Savy presumed that the "great Discoveries" he could make concerning the designs of Spain would "be so highly advantageous to the Court, as to obtain his Majesty's Grace and Favour."[37] He even offered to advise his compatriots on how they could take Saint Augustine and Havana in the event of a war.[38] In the meantime, the Spanish plot, in addition to frightening the English in the Southeast, eventually was a source of embarrassment to the Spanish crown as the details of it became known to the English government.

Trade in the Southeast
1731-1738

In the Southeast, as in many other parts of the New World, illicit trade flourished between the English and Spaniards despite the Spanish trade restrictions, the treaties, and here the dispute over Georgia. The English colonists, especially in South Carolina and Georgia, traded with the Spanish colony at Saint Augustine. Moreover, New York and other Northeastern colonies enjoyed a traffic with the Florida colony too.

For the Spanish Floridians did not limit their illicit commerce to South Carolina and Georgia nor even to the Southeast.

Spanish Florida was essentially a frontier outpost and never became self-sustaining—although the colony was able at times to supplement its *situado* (subsidy) by means of its native industries. Dependent on outside sources, the colony was chronically in want, in spite of its proximity to Cuba and other Spanish colonies, because it did not receive sufficient supplies from Spanish sources. Subject to neglect and even to disdain in Spain and the Empire—despite its strategic importance—Florida's *situado* was uncertain. It was slow in arriving if it arrived at all. Sometimes it did not.[39] Consequently, the authorities at Saint Augustine generally ignored the restrictions against trading with foreign colonies and welcomed the usually cheaper, superior, and available English goods.

In fact, it was not uncommon for the governor himself to be either inclined or impelled toward trade with his English neighbors. Governor Antonio de Benavides in the course of his administration (1718-1734) made the "mistake" of admitting "a schooner in a time of scarcity." The "mistake" was not forgotten. Governor Manuel de Montiano—a number of years later (1740)—received an order reminding him of Benavides' "mistake" and forbidding the importing of stores from any foreign colony (although he was later given permission by the king to obtain supplies in the French colonies).[40] The "mistake" was not uncommon, however.

In general, it appears that the English usually took the illicit goods to Saint Augustine to exchange for gold, silver, and/or the produce of the Florida colony. However, it was not unheard of for Spanish flags of truce to pick up goods while in an English port, even though the practice was illegal. For example, in 1729 the master of a Spanish ship, who had taken a group of English prisoners from Saint Augustine to Charleston, purchased goods in the English colony for himself and his crew. Whereupon the English authorities seized him for violating the Act of 1660. The Spaniard claimed that he had permission from the acting governor, Arthur Middleton, to purchase the needed supplies, but the judge was of the opinion that his purchases were excessive. Yet the Spanish master asserted that the practice was lawful and not uncommon for Spanish agents and messengers.[41]

For the most part both the Floridians and their English neighbors took advantage of the opportunities to trade and it thrived. The Spanish crown was on the whole unsuccessful in the efforts it made to stop illicit traffic in the Southeast. More often than not the English crown left it unhampered.

English schooners plying the Southeastern waters called regularly at Saint Augustine. For example, the sloop *Prince Frederick* of South Carolina (John Cowley) and the schooner *Good Hope* of South Carolina (John Frazier) both put in there at least twice in 1731. English ships calling at the Florida port as often as not returned from there to English colonial ports with a cargo of some sort. The *Prince Frederick,* for instance, returned on June 14, 1731, to Charleston from Saint Augustine with a parcel of oranges.[42] In May, 1732, the schooner *Good Hope* of South Carolina (Samuel Parsons) returned to Charleston from a voyage to the nearby Spanish colony with a parcel of fruit.[43] However, the *Mary* of New York (Abraham Kip) and *Swallow* of New York (William Joggets) both returned to New York from Florida this same year—the *Mary* twice—in ballast.[44]

In 1733 the English trade with Saint Augustine increased. The sloop *Orange* of Providence (Benjamin Austin) visited the Florida port twice, once in January—returning to Charleston with a parcel of fruit—and again in May.[45] The *Jacob* of New York (Abraham Kip) returned to that port in ballast in March, June, and November from voyages to Florida,[46] while the schooner *Port Royal* (William Lyford) returned to Charleston from voyages to Saint Augustine in mid-March, in May, and in July with a new master, Caleb Davis.[47] Captain Davis, who made the voyage from Saint Augustine in about five days, reported that five or six large ground masts and several pieces of ships were driven ashore and discovered, along with a recently dead cow, on the Gulf of Florida (Straits of Florida). At Saint Augustine the Spaniards believed that these had come from two Spanish men-of-war bound to Cádiz from Vera Cruz, according to the captain, who apparently brought no other news from the Spanish settlement.[48]

14

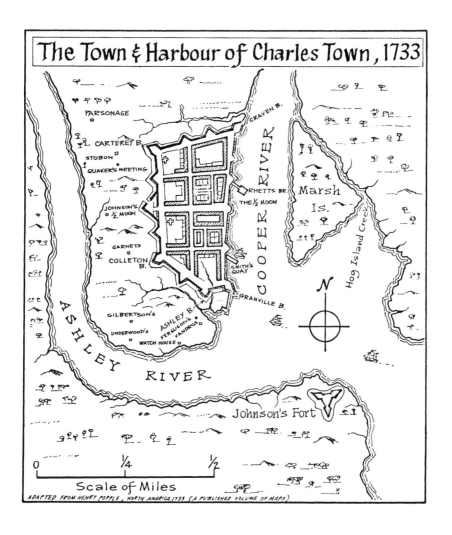

The Town & Harbour of Charles Town, 1733

PARSONAGE

CARTERET B.

STOBON

QUAKER'S MEETING

JOHNSON'S ½ MOON

GARNETS

COLLETON B.

GILBERTSON'S

UNDERWOOD'S

ASHLEY B.

FERGUSON'S

VANDROS

WATCH HOUSE

CRAVEN B.

RHETTS BR.

THE ½ MOON

SMITH'S QUAY

GRANVILLE B.

COOPER RIVER

Marsh Is.

Hog Island Creek

N

ASHLEY RIVER

Johnson's Fort

0   ¼   ½

Scale of Miles

ADAPTED FROM HENRY POPPLE, NORTH AMERICA 1733 (A PUBLISHED VOLUME OF MAPS)

English traders like Captain Caleb Davis plied the waters between their own ports and Saint Augustine on a regular basis. Eager to take full advantage of the opportunity to trade, both the English and Spanish colonists winked at all restrictions. Thus the traffic thrived.

From 1733 until 1737 the illicit trade between Charleston and Saint Augustine also increased. Four ships returned to Charleston in 1734 from voyages to Saint Augustine. The sloop *Virgins Adventure* of Port Royal (James Pollard) and (John Martyn) called at the neighboring port at least three times— returning in ballast, as did the sloop *Endeavor* of Rhode Island (Richard Waterman). The sloops *Catherine* of Jamaica (James Crawford) and *Elizabeth* of Providence (Benjamin Munroe), however, put in at Charleston after calling at Saint Augustine with cargoes of fruit, fish, and oranges.[49] The greatest flow of supplies to the Spanish colony from Charleston occurred in 1735 and 1736. Approximately fifteen different vessels took part in the traffic with Saint Augustine—all apparently English. It does not appear here that the Spaniards often sent ships to Charleston to obtain supplies, but rather that the English usually brought the illicit goods to them to exchange for gold, silver, and/or the produce of the Florida colony. Thus in 1735 the schooner *Neptune* of Charleston (Mansfield Tucker) arrived in Charleston from Saint Augustine in July, September, and November—each time with a cargo of oranges—and in the latter instance left again the following week for the Spanish colony.[50] The same week the *Neptune* departed for Saint Augustine, Sam Parsons arrived from there in the *Edward and Elizabeth.*[51] The *Neptune* returned to Charleston in January, 1736, in ballast—again returning within a fortnight to the neighboring colony.[52] This one vessel from September of 1735 through January of 1737 made about eleven voyages to and from Saint Augustine.[53]

The brigantine *Edward and Elizabeth* of Charleston (Samuel Parsons) was a fairly frequent caller at the tiny outpost too. In November, 1735, when she arrived in Charleston from Saint Augustine, she brought back a cargo of oranges. The following month (December 20, 1735) she left Charleston bound for her Spanish neighbors in Florida with a cargo of wine, vinegar, beef, corn, peas, nails, dry goods, tallow, and butter. On February 3, 1736, the *Edward and Elizabeth* arrived in Charleston from Saint Augustine with a cargo of 1000 oranges. In April of the same year, however, she returned in ballast from the neighboring port.[54]

During the one week of August 28 to September 4, 1736, three vessels, the brigantine *Edward and Elizabeth* and the sloops *Charming Betty* of Charleston (Thomas Crossthwaite) and *Rebeccah and Mary* of Charleston (William Watson) all returned from voyages to Saint Augustine.[55] The *Edward and Elizabeth* brought back to Charleston a cargo of 17,700 oranges, while the *Rebecca and Mary* brought back a cargo of about 500 oranges plus 5 or 6 deerskins and a parcel of small glasses that were apparently being returned by the Floridians. The *Charming Betty*, however, came back in ballast.[56]

Trade between the Spanish colony and Charleston thrived during this period. Authorities at Saint Augustine welcomed the English goods in spite of the Spanish restrictions. Yet there was in fact a two-way trade. For the Spanish authorities not only allowed goods to be imported from the English colonies but apparently allowed their own colonial products—oranges, for example—to be exported to the English colonies thus deliberately flaunting the Spanish trade laws.

Indeed, Francisco del Moral Sánchez, governor of Florida from 1734 to 1737, was one of the authorities who condoned the thriving traffic with the English colonies of South Carolina[57] and New York. Despite the Spanish restrictions and the strife with the English over Georgia, Moral permitted the English merchants to sell their goods in Saint Augustine. The Florida governor apparently realized the advantage of buying and/or trading Florida produce for the cheaper and generally superior English goods. Consequently the English traders peddled their goods quite freely in the Florida colony. English traders at Saint Augustine, it seems, even drove some of the Spanish merchants out of business with cheaper English goods.[58] Moral's breach of the Spanish trade laws finally led to his dismissal in 1737.[59] The crown without doubt had a strong case against the governor.

But trade between South Carolina and Spanish Florida decreased after 1736. The schooner *Neptune* which left Charleston for Saint Augustine in January, 1737, with a cargo including flour, tallow, apples, lard, wine, 4000 feet of pine boards and 7 Negroes was the sole vessel recorded as making a voyage between the two colonial ports for the entire year.[60] The following year the sloop *Charming Betty* made the only recorded—so seemingly sanctioned—voyages between Charleston and Saint Augustine in May, June, July, October, and November of 1738.[61]

The previously prospering commerce between the neighboring Southeastern colonies fell off due in large part to the English and indirectly to the Spanish. Though the English traders were seldom hesitant about violating the Spanish trade laws, and their own too for that matter, apparently the talk of war and the apprehension and fear which resulted from the Spanish plot led to restrictions on the traffic in addition to the defensive measures taken. British settlers in the Southeast—already fearful of an invasion from Havana and Saint Augustine—were subject to a prohibition against trading with their Spanish neighbor. Nevertheless, some commerce did continue, in spite of the British efforts to restrict it.

In May, 1736, Thomas Gadsden, collector of the custom house in Charleston, put a notice in the *South-Carolina Gazette,* which ran for several issues. He warned those engaged in a clandestine and illicit commerce with the Spaniards and other foreigners to cease such activity. Acting under instructions from the British commissioners of customs to enforce certain regulations concerning vessels transporting or trading goods from one river or creek to another, the collector proposed to carry out his duty.

A permit was necessary before a ship could load or take on European goods or enumerated plantation goods, or place them on shore. Gadsden, therefore, notified those concerned that if they did not, beginning the twenty-first of the month, obtain permits from his office, he would be obliged to enforce the laws. Gadsden noted too that he had credible information that a great quantity of enumerated goods recently had been loaded on vessels below the fort after first having been cleared at all the offices and then subsequently carried to foreign ports in violation of the law and to the injury of the British revenue.

17

The Charleston collector further charged that

> ... *sundry Merchants of this Place are daily concern'd in carrying on a clandestine and illegal Trade with the Spaniards and other Foreigners, all which by the duty of my Office I am obliged in the strictest manner to prevent, and therefore give the publick notice, that no persons concern'd may for the future pretend Ignorance thereof.*[62]

Several weeks after his notice first appeared, Gadsden put another notice in the *Gazette*. This time he sought to defend himself from a "few of the Trading People" of the province who had drawn up a complaint against him and presented it before the governor and council. The merchants charged that the officers of his majesty's customs had in recent years fluctuated, multiplied, and increased their fees, to which charge the collector gave an answer and offered proofs to the contrary. Answering for himself, the collector said that for thirteen years he had carried out his duties without complaints. But having some intimation of plans to present a complaint to the commissioners of his majesty's customs, he expressed the hope that the "Trading people" would treat him fairly and give him a copy soon enough so that he might send an answer by the same ship in order to vindicate himself.[63] There was no doubt a connection between the collector's warning regarding illicit commerce and the merchants' complaint against the collector, which appeared so soon after the collector's initial notice. It indicates the reluctancy of many English merchants to give up the profitable trade with their Spanish neighbors.

In February, 1737, however, the general assembly of South Carolina empowered Lieutenant Governor Thomas Broughton with the advice and consent of his council to issue an embargo to prohibit and prevent the sailing of any ships or vessels from the province during that session of the assembly. The lieutenant governor and the council also had the power to impress any ships, vessels, men, mariners, laborers, horses, arms and ammunition; and to prohibit the exportation of the provisions indicated at any time during the said session. South Carolina ports received notice of the embargo, as did the neighboring provinces. The embargo was the result of several "advices of great Consequence" which made it "highly necessary" to

18

prepare defenses against a possible sudden attack.[64] These "advises" doubtlessly stemmed from the Spanish plot against Georgia which so alarmed the English in the Southeast during this period.

In spite of the apprehension of an impending invasion by the Spaniards, there were still some South Carolinians violating the restrictions against any trade with the Spaniards. The same winter (1737), for example, several persons suspected of carrying on an illicit traffic—contrary to the interests of South Carolina at that juncture—came under close examination and steps were taken to apprehend others who had gotten away. Of the latter, a Captain Davis, supposedly was "so much for the Interest of the S_____s," that he had agreed to supply them a quantity of all kinds of provisions. Apprehended and arrested at Port Royal by order of the South Carolina government, his "sordid Principles of Self-Interest" were such that despite the fact that another man gave his word of honor for him that he would not sail, Captain Davis sailed that very same night. The South Carolina authorities—convinced of their suspicions of his "intelligence" with the "S_____s,"—sought a stricter "Inquiry into his Conduct."[65]

Hence in the Southeast the mere rumors of the Spanish plot had very real consequences for the English colonists. In addition to the defensive measures and the trade restrictions, South Carolina, for example, experienced a great scarcity of provisions resulting in an exorbitant rise in prices.[66] The merchants raised the price of rice considerably because of the embargo laid on all ships trading to Carolina, "to defend themselves in case they should be attacked by the Spaniards."[67] There was also a great scarcity of money in South Carolina,[68] perhaps, in part, because the English traders were no longer free to sell their goods at Saint Augustine in exchange for gold and silver and/or the products of the Florida colony.

The Spaniards in Saint Augustine felt the effects of the Spanish plot too. After 1736 there was the decline in the flow of goods to the Spanish colony from her Southeastern neighbors in South Carolina due apparently to the British restrictions and perhaps also to the dismissal of Moral for allowing the trade during his administration. Although some

19

commerce still continued between the two colonies in violation of both Spanish and British regulations, the Carolinians now made every effort to enforce their restrictions.

The English tried to overawe their smaller Spanish neighbor too. In April, 1737, two British men-of-war, the *Rose* and the *Shark*, visited the Florida colony. The English warships anchored at the bar of Saint Augustine at night, and the Spaniards, very surprised to see them in the morning, immediately fired the alarm guns and ordered out the cavalry. The Floridians met the man-of-war's boat in a launch with a flag of truce. Nearing the British, they lowered the flag of truce, but then hoisted it again, and came up to receive the letter for their governor who immediately called a council of war before sending a reply in the afternoon to the South Carolina governor. The contents were not made public in Charleston, but the reports were that the Spaniards complained of the warlike preparations of the English in a period of peace,

> . . . *when (as they say, and what if they could persuade us to believe it!) they have no Design against us. But, thanks to the wise Precautions our Government has taken, we are now perhaps less afraid of them than they are of us:*[69]

Despite this tension in the Southeast, relations here between individual Spaniards and Englishmen were sometimes most cordial. In June, 1737, a gentleman of Charleston, who had been in Saint Augustine for his "private affairs," reported on his return that there was a new governor in Florida. The Spanish governor treated him quite civilly, promising that he would receive justice in his affairs but ordering him to sleep on board his ship as he did not have the power of granting him full liberty to stay in town.[70] The nature of the gentleman's affairs were not indicated, however. Most likely they involved the illicit trade between the two colonies.

The same summer a Captain Farra—shipwrecked on a voyage from Jamaica to Charleston within the Cape of Florida —found himself cast away among cannibal Indians. The Indians, however, were "extremely kind" and aided the English captain in saving his cargo, rigging, etc. Upon hearing of the wreck, the Spaniards at Saint Augustine sent several small vessels to carry what was saved to their port. There the Floridians permitted Captain Farra to hire a Rhode Island sloop to carry his cargo away[71]—indicating that some commerce existed with that English colony.

But there were additional indications of a thriving trade between Saint Augustine and some of the Northeastern English colonies. In August, 1738, the governor of Florida, Manuel de Montiano, sent a letter to the governor of Cuba, Juan Francisco de Güemes y Horcasitas. Montiano assured the governor at Havana that he would not fail in any point to "display the utmost vigilance" for the safety of the Florida garrison. Therefore, Montiano told Güemes that he had requested the purveyor at New York to send him as quickly as possible supplies for one year, because "from now on those needed by the King, and designated by you can not be obtained through other channels."[72] It was rather ironic that Montiano, apprehensive about the safety of Florida, still felt compelled to seek his supplies from English sources—in this case New York.

Unable, however, to secure sufficient supplies elsewhere—including South Carolina—Montiano sought and secured them from the English in New York. For, it appears the trade between Spanish Florida and New York began to pick up in 1736 —the same year that the trade between Spanish Florida and South Carolina began to fall off. From 1734-1736, approximately thirty-four ships called at Saint Augustine from Charleston, but only six from New York. Yet in the period from 1737-1739, approximately twenty ships called at Saint Augustine from New York, but only a half dozen or so from Charleston.[73]

Commerce between New York and Saint Augustine was not unlike that between Charleston and Saint Augustine. Here, too, the Floridians not only imported but exported goods. For example, the *Don Carlos* of New York (Abraham Kip) returned on March 24, 1738, from Saint Augustine with a cargo of succads (sweetmeats of candied fruit or vegetable products) ; while the *Dom Phillip* of New York (Lewis Thibon) returned on October 31, 1738, from Saint Augustine with a cargo that included three casks of oranges.[74]

The traffic suggests that the English in the Northeast had

few qualms about trading with Saint Augustine despite the skittishness of their fellow Englishmen in the Southeast over the threat of an impending invasion by the Spaniards. On the contrary the New Yorkers were apparently eager to step in and strengthen their economic ties with the Spanish colony. No doubt the Floridians gladly welcomed them.

War between Great Britain and Spain often placed the Spaniards at Saint Augustine in a vulnerable position—especially with regard to supplies. Even the mere threat of hostilities was enough to curtail the trade in the Southeast. Thus Saint Augustine welcomed the news of the sudden suspension of the Spanish expedition against Georgia in 1735 and the decision to negotiate the boundary dispute. In fact, the Floridians "jubilantly" and "joyously" proclaimed the news through the streets of their colony.[75] For despite the Spanish trade laws Spanish Florida looked to the English colonies in the Southeast and/or Northeast for much-needed supplies. When England was at war with Spain and restricted the traffic with Saint Augustine, the Spanish colony suffered. The War of Jenkins' Ear and the closing stages of the French and Indian War showed how dependent the Floridians had become on their English neighbors.

The Orange Industry at Saint Augustine
1717-1739

Trade with the nearby English colonies in the early part of the eighteenth century meant that Spanish Florida was no longer solely dependent upon Spanish sources for much-needed supplies. Fortunately, too, the Floridians in this period were not without a productive and profitable enterprise within their own colony. With or without the usually unreliable *situado*—since oftentimes it arrived late or not at all—the Florida colonists were able to trade with the English colonists. Thus the Florida colony was no longer solely dependent economically upon the *situado*.

Spanish Florida exported vast amounts of oranges—the first Florida oranges—to her English neighbors. As early as 1717 the sloop *Swan and Eagle* of Carolina (John Dolton) brought back to Charleston a load of oranges[76] from neighboring Saint Augustine. By the decade of the 1730's, the orange trade apparently was at its peak. English vessels calling at the Florida colony went back to their own colonies laden with the golden fruit. Cargoes of 500, 1000, 17,700, or 28,000 oranges were not unheard of. In fact, English colonists as far away as New York and Philadelphia were able to enjoy the Florida fruit.[77]

In Florida, as in other parts of the New World, the "staunch" Spanish settlers often had "to rely on their own resources."[78] Here the Spaniards, frequently impelled by the absence or delay of any subsidy, apparently took full advantage of the opportunity to export the easily available produce of their own colony. For the Floridians, the orange trade was a welcome supplement to—and at times a substitute for—the *situado*.

Credit for the introduction of the orange into Florida and into the rest of the New World belongs to the Spaniards. It was Christopher Columbus who brought the first seeds from the Old World to the New. On his second voyage (1493) he took from the Canary Islands to Española the seeds of the first oranges to be grown in the New World.[79] Sometime in the sixteenth century the orange made its appearance in Florida —along with grapes, figs, various other fruits and crops, and also "considerable numbers" of cattle, horses, fowls, and hogs.[80]

In Florida—as, for example, in the West Indies—the orange thrived. Moreover, it grew easily in the area of Saint Augustine itself. Although introduced into the area by seed rather than by grafted or layered plants, this was not a handicap in the case of the orange. Unlike most major tree fruits, the seedlings of oranges will not produce inferior plants. Instead, the citrus group along with one type of mango are the only significant tree fruits that, in most instances, will develop true from seedlings.[81] Nor was the area around Saint Augustine unsuited for the cultivation of oranges. In spite of the sandy soil, the area was "far from being unproductive."[82] Early in the nineteenth century an observer noted that the soil around Saint Augustine "bears two crops of Indian corn some years, and garden vegetables always in great perfection." Orange and lemon trees grew "without cultivation" producing larger and better fruit than in Spain and Portugal.[83] Indeed the island of Santa Anastasia opposite Saint Augustine was known for the "flavour of the oranges."[84]

> *Certain it is that St. Augustine and its environs gradually became one vast orange grove, with schooners carrying loads of the golden fruit to the northern coastal cities over 200 years ago.*[85]

Unfortunately the orange trade apparently was shortlived. Interrupted by the War of Jenkins' Ear, the trade disappeared. One possible explanation is that South Carolina—a major importer—began to cultivate her own oranges. Orange trees graced the gardens of Charleston as early as 1732.[86] Moreover, South Carolina cultivated oranges to the extent that the colony began exporting them. From November 1, 1758, to November 1, 1759, for example, the port of Charleston exported some 418 barrels of its own golden fruit.[87] By the 1760's Georgia, too, was in the orange trade as an exporter of orange juice.[88] Ironically the orange groves in Carolina and Georgia that gave rise to the orange industries there probably got their start from parent oranges imported from Spanish Florida. Competition, therefore, from orange growers in nearby colonies—English and Spanish too—perhaps cut into the market for the Florida orange.

Attempts to Resolve Differences

Attempts to resolve the Anglo-Spanish differences with respect to the free navigation-contraband trade controversy and the dispute over Georgia through diplomatic channels were ultimately unsuccessful resulting in the War of Jenkins' Ear (1739). The Spanish government was unwilling to relinquish its claim to Georgia, and, in addition, continued to search and seize English vessels in order to prevent illicit commerce with the Spanish colonies. The English merchants in turn complained to their government about the Spanish "depredations," while the Georgia interests were determined that Georgia should be English. The resulting pressures finally forced the peace-loving Walpole into the war with Spain. Up until the early part of 1739, however, Great Britain and Spain made efforts to negotiate their differences.

In October, 1731, *The Political State* reported that Parliament had on order met in a committee of the whole House to consider the petitions of the Bristol and Liverpool merchants with regard to the Spanish depredations and to hear counsel for the petitioners and to examine several captains and owners of ships. The captains and owners told of over a thousand ships being taken or plundered by the Spaniards, without, according to them "any just Pretence of their having been carrying on a contraband Trade with any of the Spanish Dominions."[89] After hearing the testimony, the committee made two resolutions. The first stated that the petitioners had proved the allegations. The second expressed the opinion that the House should present an address to the king asking him to continue his endeavors to prevent Spanish depredations in the future, to obtain full satisfaction for the damages sustained, and to ensure for the subjects of Great Britain "the full and uninterrupted Exercise of their Trade and Navigation to and from the British Colonies in America."[90] The House then resolved that such an address ought to be presented to the king.[91]

Subsequently, the English minister to Spain, Benjamin Keene, complained to the Spanish court that contrary to royal orders Spanish privateers in America continued to commit hostile acts against the English and their ships on pretense of preventing illicit commerce. Keene charged that not only those with commissions from Spanish colonial governors, but others without any commissions were guilty of the depredations. The English minister further charged that the governors would not attend to the complaints of the English who suffered such unjust annoyances nor would these governors provide satisfaction for the damages.

In January, 1732, Philip V directed a *cédula* (royal order in Council) to his colonial governors regarding the alleged depredations. The Spanish king commanded the governors of his American dominions not to allow any of his subjects to molest or abuse the English or their vessels in the American waters in such latitudes where they could navigate, provided that they were not "*concerned in any illicit Commerce.*"[92] (Italics mine.) This latter condition was crucial and made the *cédula* essentially meaningless. For the English merchants did not intend nor did they in fact give up their profitable illicit trade within the Spanish Empire. Therefore the Spanish crown felt it was necessary to allow her *guardacostas* or privateers to continue searching and seizing English vessels supposedly to prevent the illicit traffic. The *cédula* further instructed the Spanish governors to enforce the royal laws and ordinances relating to the matter and to punish all those who took "unlawful" prizes. A ship caught in illicit commerce was naturally a lawful prize. Philip V ordered his governors to hear and receive complaints from English officers or commanders and to administer them justice and satisfaction for losses "unjustly sustained." Philip advised his governors that they were

> . . . to understand, that they shall be answerable for the Violences which the said Cruizers shall commit, in regard that, before they give them Commissions to go to Sea, they ought to examine into the Character of their Persons, and take security of them to their satisfaction.[93]

This *cédula*, of course, did nothing to resolve the free navigation-contraband trade controversy.

Prior to 1739, other attempts to resolve these differences were no more successful. Early in 1732, for example, English and Spanish representatives met for the first time to adjust the differences between the merchants of the two nations and agreed to meet twice each week to settle them. Both sides appeared in earnest. Consequently, there were hopes that they would "at last finish what they were sent about."[94] But a Jamaican merchant wrote to a friend in London that very year giving an account of the island and noting "the advantageous Situation of it in Time of Peace for Trade to *New Spain*,"[95] —surely an indication of the true intentions of many English merchants and of a basic cause of the dispute with Spain.

Conferences held in Spain late in 1732 between Keene and the Spanish ministers did result, however, in an agreement to send joint orders to the West Indies to cease hostilities on both sides. Jamaica, for example, also received orders to restore the register ship last taken by the English;[96] while Spain agreed to increase for an additional three years the term for the commission appointed to adjust the differences between Spain and England regarding the depredations of the Spaniards on ships belonging to English merchants.[97] But the commission did not succeed in its purpose. In 1736 at the interposition of the king of England the king of Spain once again sent orders to the West Indies to cease all hostilities there.[98]

In 1737, English merchants again petitioned the king to obtain satisfaction for their grievances. They complained that the Spaniards continued to take and plunder their ships in the West Indies. The merchants claimed that Spaniards fitted out to cruise on the "plausible Pretence" of guarding their coasts frequently stopped, searched, and "forcibly and arbitrarily" seized English vessels. The merchants also charged the Spaniards with carrying English ships into Spanish ports and condemning them along with their cargoes in violation of the treaties between England and Spain.[99]

Parliament received petitions complaining of Spanish depredations once again in March, 1738, from various merchants, planters, and others engaged in trade to the English colonies.[100] Later in the year the House of Commons responded to the complaints by passing a resolution expressing the opinion that English subjects had the "natural and undoubted" right to sail their ships in any part of the American seas to and from the various English dominions. The legislators accused the Spanish of violating this freedom of navigation and commerce on groundless and unwarrantable pretenses. They charged the Spaniards with unjust seizures and captures, attended often with "unheard of Cruelty and Barbarity."[101] The resolution further charged that applications to the Spanish court for justice and satisfaction proved ineffective, and that the Spanish governors completely ignored or evaded royal orders and *cédulas* for restitution and reparation.[102]

Philip V, of course, denied that his governors in America evaded his orders. The Spanish king insisted that the very treaties upon which the English founded their demands for "Reparation and future Security" were contrary to the demands that the English made. Moreover, the Spanish king also charged that British subjects eluded the advantage of restitution and under pretense of demanding it sent men-of-war to the

West Indies loaded with goods for the purpose of carrying on an illicit commerce.[103] Spain insisted that she had a right to obtain satisfaction from the English, who, contrary to the tenor of the treaties between them, kept every year in America over forty interloping ships of fifty to two hundred tons and asserted that these ships, on the pretense of trading with the English colonies, landed "great quantities" of goods on the coasts of the Spanish-American colonies. In exchange, the English obtained bars of silver or pieces of eight. The Dutch, accused of the same practice, admitted that the charges were not entirely groundless. In fact, the Dutch reported that there were those who did not hesitate to say,

> . . . that England has not suffered so much by the Capture of 138 Ships which the Spanish have carried to the Havanna, or any other Port of their Dominions, as it gets in one Year only from the contraband Trade in America.[104]

Finally, in July, 1738, Charleston received news that Parliament felt an open rupture with Spain was unavoidable since satisfaction for the Spanish depredations could not be obtained amicably.[105] Undoubtedly, this added to the apprehension and anxiety of the English in the Southeast—already sparked by reports of the Spanish plot against Georgia. Savannah, in August of the same year, learned that the Spaniards were again taking possession of Saint Juan where they had a fort under construction and a vessel cruising in attendance. It appeared to the Georgians to be the first step in an intended invasion—so long expected by them—which being unopposed would be succeeded by others.[106]

Failure of the Convention of Pardo

Spain and Great Britain made one final but unsuccessful attempt to peacefully resolve their differences with respect to the free navigation-contraband trade controversy and the dispute over Georgia. On January 14, 1739, representatives of the two countries signed the ill-fated Convention of Pardo. Meetings were to be held in Madrid to settle the differences over the alleged depredations and the southern boundary.[107] Spain

28

wanted to discuss Georgia first since she felt herself the injured party in that dispute due to the English advances under Oglethorpe. England, however, wanted to discuss first the differences over navigation where she believed herself to be the injured party.[108] Negotiations ultimately broke down and the pressure of the English merchants, the imperialists, and the Georgia interests finally forced the peace-loving Walpole into a war with Spain.[109]

FOOTNOTES

CHAPTER II

TRADE AND THE DEVELOPMENT OF AN ORANGE INDUSTRY IN FLORIDA, 1717-1739

1. Lanning, *Diplomatic History of Georgia*, p. 126.

2. Frances Gardiner Davenport, ed., *European Treaties Bearing on the History of the United States and its Dependencies*, II (Washington, D.C., 1929), 188-89.

3. Edward W. Lawson, "What Became of the Man Who Cut Off Jenkins' Ear?" *Florida Historical Quarterly*, XXXVII (July, 1958 — April, 1959), 33. (Hereafter cited as Lawson, "Jenkins' Ear?")

4. *Ibid.*

5. B. R. Carroll, comp., *Historical Collections of South Carolina: Embracing Many Rare and Valuable Pamphlets and Other Documents Relating to the History of the State from its Discovery to its Independence*, I (New York, 1836), 326-29.

6. *Gazette*, March 4-11, 1732.

7. Lawson, "Jenkins' Ear?" pp. 34-35.

8. *Gazette*, March 4-11, 1732.

9. *Gazette*, January 22-29, 1732.

10. *Gazette*, September 16-23, 1732.

11. *Gazette*, November 4-11, 1732.

12. *Gazette*, December 2-9, 1732.

13. *Gazette*, January 20-27, 1735.

14. Lanning, *Diplomatic History of Georgia*, pp. 2-3.

15. *Ibid.*, p. 1.

16. *Gazette*, May 17-24, 1735.

17. *Gazette*, November 9-16, 1734.

18. Lanning, *Diplomatic History of Georgia*, p. 220.

19. *Ibid.*, pp. 50, 221.

20. *Ibid.*, p. 56.

21. *Ibid.*, p. 59.

22. *Ibid.*, p. 80.

23. *Ibid.*, pp. 75-76.

24. *Gazette*, November 6-13, 1736.

25. *Gazette*, December 18-24, 1736.

26. *Gazette*, February 12-19, February 19-26, 1737.

27. *Gazette*, February 12-19, 1737.

28. J. H. Easterby, ed., *The Colonial Records of South Carolina: Journal of the Commons House of Assembly, November 10, 1736 — June 7, 1739* (Columbia, 1951), p. 230. (Hereafter cited as Easterby, *Colonial Records of South Carolina, 1736-1739.*)

29. *Ibid.*, pp. 248-49.

30. *Gazette*, February 19-26, 1737.

31. *Gazette*, May 28 - June 4, 1737.

32. *Gazette*, June 18-25, 1737.

33. Lanning, *Diplomatic History of Georgia*, p. 80.

34. *Gazette*, April 15, 1738.

35. Lanning, *Diplomatic History of Georgia*, p. 82.

36. *Ibid.*, p. 80.

37. *Gazette*, February 9-16, 1738.

38. Lanning, *Diplomatic History of Georgia*, p. 79.

39. TePaske, *Governorship of Spanish Florida*, p. 228; Charles W. Arnade, "Cattle Raising in Spanish Florida, 1513-1763," *Agricultural History*, XXXV (July, 1961), 117.

40. *Collections of the Georgia Historical Society*, Vol. VII, pt. I (Savannah, 1909), No. 205, Letter, Manuel de Montiano to Juan Francisco de Güemes y Horcasitas, July 28, 1740. (Hereafter cited as *Collections.*)

41. Dorothy S. Towle, ed., *Records of the Vice-Admiralty Court of Rhode Island, 1716-1752*, American Legal Records, Vol. III (Washington, D.C., 1936), p. 55.

42. Great Britain, Public Record Office MSS, Colonial Office, South Carolina (hereafter cited as CO/SC), 5: 509, fols. 79-81, 96, Shipping Returns, March 31, May 17, June 14, October 21, 1731. A name within a parenthesis following the name of a ship indicates the master of the ship.

43. CO/SC, 5: 509, fol. 115, Shipping Returns, May 13, 1732; *Gazette*, May 13-20, 1732.

44. Great Britain, Public Record Office MSS, Colonial Office, New York (hereafter cited as CO/NY), 5: 1225, pt. 1, fols. 35, 47, 58, Shipping Returns, May 24, August 2, October 9, 1732.

45. CO/SC, 5: 509, fol. 113, Shipping Returns, January 31, 1733; *Gazette*, January 27 - February 3, May 5-12, 1733.

46. CO/NY, 5: 1225, pt. 1, fols. 68, 88, 104, Shipping Returns, March 23, June 25, November 28, 1733.

47. *Gazette*, March 24-31, May 19-26, July 28 - August 4, 1733.

48. *Gazette*, July 28 - August 4, 1733.

49. CO/SC, 5: 509, fols. 122, 128, 132, 138, 139, Shipping Returns,

January 21, June 10, July 17, 1734, January 20, February 10, 1735; *Gazette*, April 13-20, July 13-20, November 30 - December 7, 1734.

50. CO/SC, 5: 509, fols. 151, 152, 153, Shipping Returns, July 7, September 4, November 8, 1735; *Gazette*, November 8-15, November 15-22, 1735.

51. CO/SC, 5: 509, fol. 153, Shipping Returns, November 20, 1735; *Gazette*, November 15-22, 1735.

52. CO/SC, 5: 510, fol. 11, Shipping Returns, January 16, 1736; *Gazette*, January 10-17, January 31 - February 7, 1736.

53. *Gazette*, November 8-15, November 15-22, November 22-29, 1735; January 10-17, January 31 - February 7, March 6-13, May 15-22, September 25 - October 2, December 4-11, 1736.

54. CO/SC, 5: 509, fols. 152, 153, Shipping Returns, November 20, December 20, 1735; CO/SC, 5: 510, fols. 1, 11, Shipping Returns, February 3, April 22, 1736.

55. *Gazette*, August 28 - September 4, 1736.

56. CO/SC, 5: 510, fol. 7, Shipping Returns, September 2, 1736.

57. TePaske, *Governorship of Spanish Florida*, pp. 88-89.

58. *Ibid.*

59. John Jay TePaske, "Economic Problems of the Florida Governors," *Florida Historical Quarterly*, XXXVI (September, 1958), 49. (Hereafter cited as TePaske, "Economic Problems.")

60. CO/SC, 5: 510, fol. 26, Shipping Returns, January 25, 1737; *Gazette*, January 8-15, 1737.

61. *Gazette*, June 1, July 6, October 12, November 16, 1738.

62. *Gazette*, May 8-15, 1736.

63. *Gazette*, May 29 - June 5, 1736.

64. *Gazette*, February 5-12, 1737.

65. *Ibid.*

66. *Gazette*, March 12-19, 1737.

67. *Gazette*, July 30 - August 6, 1737.

68. *Gazette*, March 12-19, 1737.

69. *Gazette*, April 16-23, 1737.

70. *Gazette*, June 18-25, 1737.

71. *Gazette*, August 20-27, 1737.

72. *Collections*, No. 76, Letter, Manuel de Montiano to Juan Francisco de Güemes y Horcasitas, August 31, 1738.

73. CO/SC, 5: 509, fols. 122, 128, 132, 138, 139, 146, 151-53, Shipping Returns, 1734-1736; CO/SC, 5: 510, fols. 1, 3, 7, 11, 13, 26, 27, 35, Shipping Returns, 1736-1739; CO/NY, 5: 1225, pt. 1, fols. 121, 149, pt. 2, 156, 160, 168, 175, 196, 264, Shipping Returns, 1734-1737; CO/NY, 5: 1226, fols. 2-3, 7, 10, 12-13, 39, 44, 53, 69, Shipping Returns, 1738-1739; CO/NY, 5: 1227, fols. 2, 24, 47, Shipping Returns, 1739; Customs Records, *Gazette*, 1734-1739.

74. CO/NY, 5: 1226, fols. 2, 13, Shipping Returns, March 24, October 31, 1738.

75. Lanning, *Diplomatic History of Georgia*, p. 50.

76. CO/SC, 5: 508, fol. 32, Shipping Returns, December 25, 1717.

77. CO/SC, 5: 509, fol. 153, Shipping Returns, October 21, 1735;

CO/SC, 5: 510, fols. 7, 11, Shipping Returns, February 3, September 2, 1736; CO/NY, 5: 1226, fol. 13, Shipping Returns, October 31, 1738.

78. Dario Fernández-Flórez, *The Spanish Heritage in the United States* (Madrid, 1965), p. 297.

79. Ralph T. Robinson, "Some Aspects of the History of Citrus in Florida," *Quarterly Journal of the Florida Academy of Sciences*, VIII (March, 1945), 59. (Hereafter cited as Robinson, "Citrus in Florida.")

80. Verne E. Chatelain, "Spanish Contributions in Florida to American Culture," *Florida Historical Quarterly*, XIX (January, 1941), 237. (Hereafter cited as Chatelain, "Spanish Contributions.")

81. Robinson, "Citrus in Florida," pp. 60-61.

82. James Grant Forbes, *Sketches, Historical and Topographical, of the Floridas: More Particularly of East Florida* (Gainesville, 1964), p. 88. (Hereafter cited as Forbes, *Sketches*.)

83. Forbes, *Sketches*, p. 88.

84. *Ibid.*, p. 89.

85. Robinson, "Citrus in Florida," p. 60.

86. *Gazette*, January 20 - January 27, 1732.

87. *South Carolina Weekly Gazette* (Charleston), October 24 - October 31, 1759.

88. Bernard Romans, *A Concise Natural History of East and West Florida* (Gainesville, 1962), p. 104. See chart "AN AGGREGATE and VALUATION of EXPORTS of PRODUCE from the PROVINCE of GEORGIA, with the NUMBER of VESSELS and TONNAGE employed therein, annually distinguished, from the Year 1754, to 1773," compiled by William Brown, Comptroller and Searcher of his Majesty's Customs in the port of Savannah.

89. *Gazette*, April 22-29, 1732.

90. *Ibid.*

91. *Ibid.*

92. *Gazette*, April 29 - May 6, 1732.

93. *Ibid.*

94. *Gazette*, May 27-31, 1732.

95. *Gazette*, June 24 - July 1, 1732.

96. *Gazette*, March 17-24, 1733.

97. *Gazette*, April 28 - May 5, 1733.

98. *Gazette*, October 9-16, 1736.

99. *Gazette*, January 5-12, 1738.

100. *Gazette*, July 27, 1738.

101. *Gazette*, August 10, 1738.

102. *Ibid.*

103. *Gazette*, October 19, 1738.

104. *Gazette*, February 9-16, 1738.

105. *Gazette*, July 6, 1738.

106. *Gazette*, August 24, 1738.

107. Lanning, *Diplomatic History of Georgia*, p. 149.

108. *Ibid.*, p. 84.

109. *Ibid.*, p. 173.

CHAPTER III

THE WAR OF JENKINS' EAR
STIMULATES PRIVATEERING,
1739-1748

The War of Jenkins' Ear began October 23, 1739. In Europe, this conflict between Spain and England merged into the War of the Austrian Succession. In America, the entrance of France in 1744 reopened hostilities between the French and English colonies and developed into King George's War. The fighting in both Europe and America lasted until the signing of the Treaty of Aix-la-Chapelle in 1748.

In the Southeast, the War of Jenkins' Ear meant the renewal of open war between the English colonies and Spanish Florida. The English, especially in South Carolina and Georgia, feared invasion by the Spaniards, who likewise feared invasion by the English. Each side made unsuccessful attempts against the other. James Oglethorpe led two expeditions to Saint Augustine in 1740 and 1743. The English stopped the Spaniards at Bloody Marsh when they invaded Georgia in 1742. Privateering, which began before the formal declaration of war, flourished off the Southeastern coast as it did in the rest of America, the West Indies, and Europe.

Despite the war, illicit trade continued between the neighboring colonies. Their flag of truce ships—used for the exchange of prisoners—were convenient instruments for the traffic. But oftentimes individual captains called at Spanish colonial ports without any pretense—except to sell illicit articles of trade.

Privateering

After the Convention of Pardo failed to solve the differences over the problems between the English and Spanish in the

33

colonies, Great Britain took sterner measures against the Spaniards making war inevitable. Prior to the actual rupture with Spain, the British government directed her colonial governors to issue commissions of marque and reprisal for fitting out private ships of war. These privateers were to seize the vessels and goods of the king of Spain in retaliation for the Spanish depredations. The English colonists also were under strict orders not to supply the Spaniards with ammunitions or stores of any kind. William Bull, the lieutenant governor of South Carolina, issued a proclamation containing these instructions in September, 1739,[1] likewise, the other English colonial governors issued similar instructions. To prevent the Spaniards gaining any supplies from them,[2] Admiral Edward Vernon gave orders early in 1740 for the British ships in the West Indies to search all English privateers to see that they carried no more than four months' provisions.

In the eighteenth century, the various governments of Europe legalized the profession of privateering.[3] Though privately owned and manned, privateers had commissions (letters of marque and reprisal) from their government to commit acts of warfare on enemy vessels. Privateering was, of course, subject to much abuse, and the leading powers in Europe finally agreed to abandon it in 1856 (Declaration of Paris).[4] During the War of Jenkins' Ear, however, privateering was still common practice and the West Indies swarmed with the sails of national fleets and privately-armed vessels.[5] The life of a privateersman offered both adventure and risk[6] as well as profit, and the English and Spaniards encouraged it—the latter often compelled by their need for supplies.

There were many ways to stimulate privateering. In 1740, for example, the South Carolina general assembly, upon petition of a Jamaican privateersman, agreed to remit the duties and customs on goods captured from the Spanish and brought into the port of Charleston. To encourage privateers and the regular navy,[7]—the petitioner pointed out at the time—the British government already had remitted all such duties on captured goods. Then in 1741 the general assembly of South Carolina voted to pay Captain John Rowse, of the privateer sloop *Speedwell,* five pounds sterling per head for Spanish prisoners taken between

Cape Hatteras and Cape Florida and brought into Charleston. The assembly also granted him a quantity of gunpowder. Some merchants and other citizens of Charleston had contracted with Captain Rowse—at considerable expense—to protect their ships along the coast and had requested that the South Carolina government encourage Rowse to be diligent in performing his contracts.[8] Rowse seemed faithful. He shortly returned to Charleston with a Spanish privateer sloop with nineteen hands, which he had taken three days out of Saint Augustine. The same day the privateer *Phenix* returned *"With his usual Success,* he having been out some weeks past and luckily met with no Enemy" the *South-Carolina Gazette* pointed out somewhat sarcastically with respect to his majesty's ship *Phenix*. The *Gazette* applauded the success of the South Carolinian privateer commanded by Captain Rowse, however.

> *We now begin to hope that Capt. Rouss's [Rowse] Vigilance and Courage will spoil the Spaniards future Gleanings, they have made but too good a Harvest already; which Hopes would be greatly enlarged should either the Country or the Merchants fit out 2 or 3 Privateers—Commanders more of Capt. Rouss's Spirit and Activity.[9]*

In the fall of 1744 the *Gazette* reported that before winter there would be an estimated 113 privateers afloat, based in Britain's American colonies, the majority of which were stout vessels and well manned.[10] Havana, alone, in 1746, reportedly had 17 privateers preparing to cruise on the British-American coasts during the summer.[11]

The Southeast contributed its share of privateers during the war. North Carolina in July, 1741, fitted out two vessels to go after the Spanish privateers infesting her coasts.[12] The same summer James Oglethorpe sent out his guard sloop and two privateers from Georgia to cruise off Saint Augustine.[13] South Carolina, of course, also had her privateers. The *Isabella,* a captured Spanish half galley (the only large one the Spaniards had in America), the *Mercury,* and the *Alexander,* were only a few of the privateers based in the province.[14] Saint Augustine for her part sent five privateers out to cruise the Southeastern coasts in the spring of 1743.[15] Early in 1747, Saint Augustine expected two large privateers (one a schooner and the other a sloop) from Havana for cruising off the English colonial coasts.[16]

The Southeast, in the period 1739-1748, abounded with instances of privateering. Vessels were captured, sometimes two or three times, and both the Spanish and the English took many prizes. In 1742, a privateer from Georgia, on its way to Saint Augustine with a flag of truce to exchange prisoners, encountered and took into Frederica a Spanish sloop from Havana loaded with bale goods, brandy, and provisions valued at thirty thousand pounds sterling, including some pieces of eight.[17] The *Isabella* from Charleston in 1747 arrived in Providence with a considerable sum of money taken from a Spanish flag of truce on its way from Havana to Jamaica.[18] The *Cartwright* privateer, also of Charleston, took in 1748 a brigantine with wine, brandy, and bale goods bound for Saint Augustine.[19]

The Spaniards at Saint Augustine were no less successful. Three Spanish prisoners in Georgia reported thirteen English prizes in the harbor at Saint Augustine in the summer of 1741—all taken on the Southeastern coast. In the summer of 1744, a Spanish privateer took a ship bound from Charleston to Bristol, England, and carried her into Saint Augustine. The captured cargo included 101 hogsheads of deerskins, 60 barrels of rice, 196 barrels of pitch, 251 barrels of turpentine, and 149 barrels of tar.[20] In the fall of 1745, seventeen English prizes reportedly were at Saint Augustine. Several of the latter group were vessels captured en route from northern ports for Charleston; the prizes supposedly were to sail for Havana under convoy of the three Spanish privateers which had taken them.[21]

The Spaniards' audacity vexed the Southeastern English colonists considerably. For they seemed to be ubiquitous, cruising off the English colonial coasts and chasing English ships. In fact, the Spaniards were so bold as to chase English vessels within one hundred leagues of Charleston.[22] In 1741, a Spanish sloop stationed off North Carolina took a fine large sloop bound from Boston to Cape Fear and sent her into Saint Augustine where the Floridians soon fitted her out as a privateer. Three Englishmen who escaped from Saint Augustine the same year reported that the Spanish had taken and sent to Havana thirty-six vessels, the majority of which were captured on the Southeastern coast. The Spaniards themselves boasted that the English at Carolina were all certainly asleep, or else they would not allow their enemy to take English vessels even at the bar of Charleston.[23] But, in April, 1745, Spanish privateers again took vessels in sight of Charleston.[24] By July, there were reports that Julian de la Vega—plying the coast in a privateer from Saint Augustine—came up each night to the bar of Charleston.[25]

The English showed their audacity also. English colonists sent privateers such as Captain Rowse to cruise off Saint Augustine, but the war which began with France in 1744 added to the troubles of the English colonists as French privateers joined frequently with their Spanish allies in the Southeastern waters.

Though the flourishing state of privateering was doubtless profitable to some (the masters, owners, and crews of privateers for example), it was detrimental to the normal trading activities of both the English and Spanish in the Southeast. The war disturbed the trade of the English, and convoys were oftentimes necessary for the merchant vessels. Consequently, a major purpose of the English privateering was to legalize armed protection. Generally, it took the urging or financial backing of prominent merchants to accomplish this.[26]

Conditions at Saint Augustine as a Spur to Spanish Privateering

The Spaniards at Saint Augustine resorted to privateering to obtain much-needed supplies. In 1740 Spanish and Negro deserters from Saint Augustine reported that the town was very short of provisions and that many more would desert.[27] The boldness the Spaniards showed in chasing vessels within one hundred leagues of Charleston—which so annoyed the English in July, 1740—was due to sheer necessity. For Governor Manuel de Montiano wrote that same month to Captain General Juan Francisco de Güemes y Horcasitas in Cuba that my "greatest concern is for supplies, and if we get none, there is no doubt we shall die of hunger."[28] This was during the formal siege of

Saint Augustine by the English under James Oglethorpe.[29]

Letters written by the governor to the captain general prior to the formal siege, however, told of deteriorating conditions in Saint Augustine. In January, 1740, Montiano wrote that the residents there caused him much annoyance, for most of them were requesting permission to go to Havana. They complained of the lack of food and feared continuance of the problem throughout the war. The Floridians objected also to the misfortunes and privations resulting from the want of pay. Montiano and the royal officers decided, however, that for the time being no one would be allowed to move. The governor felt the grounds for the requests to go to Havana were sound, and "might induce me to send away hence all useless mouths," but the lack of information as to what state the present differences might produce kept him from approving them. He felt, too, that the king wished the province to be peopled, and it would be "very difficult to make them return once away." Montiano also noted that the burden would be extreme if Saint Augustine were besieged because of the small enclosure of the castle and the scarcity of food.[30]

Besieged by sea, Montiano wrote to Güemes on May 13, 1740, that they were in extreme want and without food. Preservation, he said, depended on supplies from Cuba because without them "it is not possible that we shall preserve our lives." He requested the captain general to supply Saint Augustine with the "greatest" possible amount of supplies in vessels which would be strong enough to cope with the three English vessels on their coast, "for in no other way do I see any help, and consequently an irreparable calamity is hanging over us."[31] By May 15, 1740, Montiano wrote that unless help came by June 20 at the latest, "it is the most natural thing in the world that this garrison perish."[32]

Later the same year, after a convoy of supplies for Saint Augustine from Cuba was lost, Montiano armed the *Campeche* sloop as a privateer. The *Campeche* departed the Florida port on October 17—later capturing a Carolina schooner which she sent back to Saint Augustine. Another vessel, captured off Charleston en route to Hamburg, had over nine thousand *arro-*

bas (quarters) of rice on board. This latter cargo arrived at the Florida port on October 28 and proved to be the salvation of Saint Augustine. The troops and entire neighborhood lived on the rice, which they baked into *roscas* (ring-shaped biscuits or cakes).

When the privateer Joseph Sánchez decided to quit his privateering and sell his sloop, Montiano bought and fitted it out. He gave the command of the ship to Don Juan de León Fandiño.[33] This was the man who cut off Jenkins' ear on April 9, 1731. Robert Jenkins, however, was not the completely innocent victim of the Spanish he pretended to be. His ship—searched by León—contained a considerable sum of Spanish gold, was overstocked with fresh provisions, and too far off course to be an innocent merchant ship. After the episode with Jenkins, León continued to annoy the English merchants.[34] He carried some supplies to Saint Augustine before the siege (1740), and after the English forces were drawn off he went out in search of English vessels laden with provisions. León took thirty-eight, before he was captured for the first time in his career by Captain Thomas Frankland of the British ship the *Rose* (June 4, 1742). This Spaniard, León, spent forty years at sea, twenty-three of them under the commission of the king of Spain. The *South-Carolina Gazette* paid him a tribute in stating after his capture that

> *he was the man generally employed to scour the Bays of Campeachy and Honduras, or to go on any desperate attempt, for which no one was more fitting, as will appear by his engaging the Rose so resolutely and long as he did.*[35]

His fate after his capture is not known.[36]

In July, 1741, letters found on board a sloop bound for Havana, but captured off Saint Augustine by the English, gave a dismal account of the lack of provisions in the Florida colony.[37] The same summer provisions reportedly were "very dear and scarce in the Havannah,"[38] where they feared a visit by Admiral Vernon. Later in the year there were reports that the governor of Cuba had sent to Saint Augustine for assistance, "from which you may judge of their condition."[39] Early in 1742, Saint Augustine was again apparently in great want because Admiral Vernon's presence in Cuba blocked that source of supply.[40] Thus sheer necessity was often the motive behind the Spanish privateering. The Spanish privateersmen—who infested the Southeastern English colonies and so vexed the merchants there— were only taking advantage of what was often their sole means of obtaining supplies for Saint Augustine.

Illicit Trade

The often-pressing need for supplies at Saint Augustine contributed also to an illicit commerce between the Spanish and English colonies in the Southeast. A cartel between Spain and Great Britain for exchanging prisoners under flags of truce, provided a convenient means for the illicit trade.[41] For in spite of the earlier orders prohibiting the export of provisions to foreign colonies, the British government learned that its North American colonists, nevertheless, exported great quantities of provisions to foreign colonies. In 1741, therefore, the British government directed its colonial governors to prevent such traffic. Ships loaded with provisions, other than those in his majesty's service, were to give sufficient security before sailing to land the provisions in some part of the British dominions. The lieutenant governor of South Carolina issued a proclamation to this effect in March, 1741.[42]

In October, 1743, the South Carolina lower house of assembly ordered a committee to inquire into any illicit commerce carried on by inhabitants of the province with Saint Augustine. Subsequently, the lower house learned that the lieutenant governor in council was already undertaking such an inquiry and wished the matter to be left to him.[43] However, the South Carolina assembly in its 1744-1745 session, again initiated inquiries into the subject of illicit trade with Spanish Florida, indicating that it had not stopped. The members expressed concern over the use of trading vessels as flags of truce, since such vessels were liable to be seized by the Spaniards or French. They also recommended that all possible care be taken to prevent any traffic being carried on by flags of truce and that they be supplied only with the bare necessities—an indication of how the trade was being carried on.[44]

During the same session (February 21, 1745) a house committee investigating the matter concluded that it was evident that an illicit commerce had been and was being carried on with the Spaniards by various South Carolinians. Testimony heard by the committee told of goods illegally loaded on a Spanish flag of truce under the command of Don Julian. William Coomer—one of the witnesses—testified under oath that he had been employed the previous year to place goods on board the said flag of truce and had in the night taken on board his schooner five pipes of wine which he then put on board the Spanish vessel. The night before the Spanish ship sailed, he placed other merchandise on board. Coomer reported, too, seeing calves, sheep, hogs, and other livestock on the deck and in the hold of the flag of truce. Other testimony told of English captains sailing to Saint Augustine with cargoes of hogs, turkeys and other poultry, flour, and, on one occasion, five Negro men who were sold for two hundred pieces of eight each. The committee recommended that action be taken to prevent such activities and that the guilty parties be prosecuted.[45] The council, however, rejected on procedural grounds the same year (March 19, 1745) a bill to prevent "clandestine trade, commerce or correspondence with His Majesty's enemies."[46]

Grievances presented by the grand jury at the Court of General Sessions in Charleston in 1745 included the "pernicious practice and underhand trade" carried on in Charleston and other Carolina ports with Saint Augustine and Havana under protection of the flags of truce. Arms, ammunition and intelligence, as well as provisions, reached the enemy via these flags of truce who neglected "to clear out at all the proper offices."[47] There were also complaints about the Spanish and French prisoners being allowed to walk around Charleston in so "publick a Manner."[48]

The illicit traffic continued throughout the war in spite of both British and Spanish restrictions. The illicit trade was, of course, risky. In May, 1745, the Spaniards seized and then sold several vessels engaged in an illicit commerce with Saint Augustine and made the crews prisoners.[49] But, in 1746, Havana reportedly was as plentifully and regularly supplied from Providence as Saint Augustine was from Carolina, yet according to the *Gazette,*

> . . . *we have never heard that any of the Offenders have been brought to Justice for those Crimes. We have lately seen Examples made (and that very justly) on some who have taken up Arms against their Prince; and why those who supply the Enemy with Provisions in Time of War (and probably with something else) Should escape with Impunity, we must leave our Betters to say.*[50]

Perhaps, a major reason for the illicit traffic during the war was that both the English and Spanish in the Southeast suffered somewhat when the trade between them was cut off. At Saint Augustine the Spaniards were in desperate need of supplies. But at Charleston there were complaints in the *Gazette* in May, 1745, of the whole country being deprived of its most useful manufactures for the sake of the profits gained by a few from the illicit commerce with his majesty's enemies.[51] South Carolina in 1746, however, was in a period of depression. Markets open to her staple products in normal times—such as the trade in rice to the southward of Cape Finisterre and the trade with Saint Augustine—were no longer open, and her revenue from the sale of rice was in a state of decline.[52] Her trade appeared to be at so low an ebb "that it may be truly said, very few or none reap the benefit thereof excepting the merchants, who deal with the *French* and *Spaniards.*" For there was little money except for the gold or silver that came in from the French and Spanish trade.[53] On the surface, therefore, it would appear that the restrictions on commerce with the Spaniards contributed to the depression in South Carolina. Indeed, the only ones prospering were those engaging in the traffic with the Spaniards at Saint Augustine and other places in spite of the wartime restrictions. Orders in February, 1748, to prepare a bill to prevent inhabitants of Charleston from trading with his majesty's enemies never proceeded beyond that state,[54] and became unnecessary when peace came later that year.

The War of Jenkins' Ear came to an end early in 1748. There were several instances of Spanish privateering on the Southeastern coasts after the formal cessation of hostilities, but before word of the peace reached the Florida colony. Quite a few of these vessels, which were carried into Saint Augustine and condemned as lawful prizes, contained valuable cargoes.[55] As late as December, 1748, the Floridians still pursued their privateering activities. The English complained of the insolence of "Our Neighbors" and expressed the hope that they would be hunted and treated as pirates.[56]

After the war, there was a resumption of the trade between South Carolina and Florida. From September to December, 1748, at least five vessels made voyages between Charleston and Saint Augustine.[57] Whether these were flags of truce exchanging remaining prisoners or traders is not certain, but there were reports in December, 1748, of several seizures of English traders at both Havana and Saint Augustine. There were also reports that Spaniards off Saint Augustine plundered some English prisoners, who were in a flag of truce headed for Charleston, of their clothes, etc.[58] It is probable that some of the above five vessels were English traders anxious to resume a more open traffic with Saint Augustine, for Spaniards at the Florida garrison soon welcomed them again. Indeed, after the war, commerce between the English and Spaniards in the Southeast once again flourished despite the restrictions. Both the Floridians and their English neighbors suffered when the war interrupted their trade—both therefore welcomed its resumption after the war.

FOOTNOTES

CHAPTER III

THE WAR OF JENKINS' EAR STIMULATES PRIVATEERING, 1739-1748

1. *Gazette*, September 8-15, 1739.
2. *Gazette*, May 24-31, 1740.
3. John Franklin Jameson, ed., *Privateering and Piracy in the*

Colonial Period: Illustrative Documents (New York, 1923), p. ix.

4. *Ibid.*

5. B. Norton, ed., "Journal of a Privateersman," *Atlantic Monthly*, July, 1861, p. 353.

6. *Ibid.*

7. J. H. Easterby, ed., *The Colonial Records of South Carolina: Journal of the Commons House of Assembly, September 12, 1739 - March 26, 1741* (Columbia, 1952), pp. 352-56.

8. J. H. Easterby, ed., *The Colonial Records of South Carolina: Journal of the Commons House of Assembly, May 18, 1741 - July 10, 1742* (Columbia, 1953), pp. 75, 77, (hereafter cited as Easterby, *Colonial Records of South Carolina, 1741-1742*) ; *Gazette*, July 16-23, 1741.

9. *Gazette*, July 16-23, 1741.

10. *Gazette*, November 26, 1744.

11. *Gazette*, November 26, 1746.

12. *Gazette*, September 12-19, 1741.

13. *Gazette*, July 9-16, 1741.

14. *Gazette*, October 18, 1746.

15. *Gazette*, May 9, 1743.

16. *Gazette*, February 9, 1747.

17. *Gazette*, February 20-27, February 27 - March 6, March 6-13, 1742.

18. *Gazette*, March 30 - April 6, 1747.

19. *Gazette*, January 25 - February 1, 1748.

20. *Gazette*, September 10, 1744; October 7, 1745.

21. *Gazette*, October 7, 1745.

22. *Gazette*, July 5-12, 1740.

23. *Gazette*, June 25 - July 2, 1741.

24. *Gazette*, April 22, 1745.

25. *Gazette*, July 22, 1745.

26. Lanning, *Diplomatic History of Georgia*, p. 189.

27. *Gazette*, April 26 - May 3, 1740.

28. *Collections*, No. 203, Letter, Manuel de Montiano to Juan Francisco de Güemes y Horcasitas, July 6, 1740.

29. *Ibid.*, No. 205, Letter, Manuel de Montiano to Juan Francisco de Güemes y Horcasitas, July 28, 1740.

30. *Ibid.*, No. 181, Letter, Manuel de Montiano to Juan Francisco de Güemes y Horcasitas, January 31, 1740.

31. *Ibid.*, No. 198, Letter, Manuel de Montiano to Juan Francisco de Güemes y Horcasitas, May 13, 1740.

32. *Ibid.*, No. 200, Letter, Manuel de Montiano to Juan Francisco de Güemes y Horcasitas, May 15, 1740.

33. *Ibid.*, No. 248, Letter, Manuel de Montiano to Juan Francisco de Güemes y Horcasitas, January 2, 1741; Montiano Letters, No. 248, Letter, Manuel de Montiano to Juan Francisco de Güemes y Horcasitas, January 2, 1741.

34. Lawson, "Jenkins' Ear?" pp. 33-41.

35. *Gazette*, June 28 - July 5, 1742.

36. Lawson, "Jenkins' Ear?" p. 33.

37. Easterby, *Colonial Records of South Carolina, 1741-1742*, p. 92.

38. *Gazette*, July 16-23, 1741.

39. *Gazette*, July 16-23, November 28 - December 5, 1741.

40. Postscript, *Gazette*, January 9, 1742.

41. Postscript, *Gazette*, February 7, 1743.

42. *Gazette*, March 5-12, 1741.

43. J. H. Easterby, ed., *The Colonial Records of South Carolina: Journal of the Commons House of Assembly, September 14, 1742 - January 27, 1744* (Columbia, 1954), pp. 470-74.

44. J. H. Easterby, ed., *The Colonial Records of South Carolina: Journal of the Commons House of Assembly, February 20, 1744 - May 25, 1745* (Columbia, 1955), p. 189.

45. *Ibid.*, pp. 353-55.

46. *Ibid.*, p. 385.

47. *Gazette*, April 15, 1745.

48. *Ibid.*

49. *Gazette*, May 25, 1745.

50. *Gazette*, September 29, 1746.

51. *Gazette*, May 18, 1745.

52. J. H. Easterby, ed., *The Colonial Records of South Carolina: Journal of the Commons House of Assembly, September 10, 1746 - June 13, 1747* (Columbia, 1958), p. viii.

53. *Gazette*, August 23, 1746.

54. J. H. Easterby, ed., *The Colonial Records of South Carolina: Journal of the Commons House of Assembly, January 19, 1748 - June 29, 1748* (Columbia, 1961), p. 85.

55. *Gazette*, October 31 - November 7, November 7-14, 1748.

56. *Gazette*, December 7-12, 1748.

57. *Gazette*, September 21, October 3-10, October 17-24, October 24-31, November 21 - December 3, December 19-26, 1748.

58. *Gazette*, December 7-12, 1748.

CHAPTER IV

FLORIDA ENJOYS A THRIVING TRADE WITH
HER ENGLISH NEIGHBORS UNTIL THE
OUTBREAK OF WAR, 1748-1763

The Treaty of Aix-la-Chapelle did not resolve the differences between the Spanish, English, and French with respect to their American colonies, nor did it end the contest for colonial dominance. Thus, after six years of uneasy peace, the French and Indian War began. This proved to be the last and most decisive of the intercolonial struggles. In contrast to the previous intercolonial wars, this one originated in America and then spread to Europe where it was known as the Seven Years' War. The hostilities in America first broke out between the English and French colonists, and it was only near the end of the war in 1762 that the Spanish entered on the side of the French.

Neither the treaty of 1748 nor the separate treaty between Spain and England signed October 5, 1750, succeeded in resolving the Spanish and English differences. Consequently, the dispute over freedom of navigation in the West Indies and the contraband trade carried on by the English with the Spanish colonies resumed not long after the War of Jenkins' Ear ended. Although Anglo-Spanish relations somewhat improved after 1748, attempts at settlement once more were ultimately unsatisfactory and grievances again mounted. Thus the year 1762 saw previously neutral Spain, by then the weakest of the three colonial powers, drawn into the French and Indian War on the side of France. This was a final and unsuccessful attempt to prevent the English from gaining colonial dominance in North America.

Contraband Trade and Freedom of Navigation

After the War of Jenkins' Ear, the English still persisted in their contraband trade with the Spanish-American colonies and complained vigorously when the "piratical" Spanish *guardacostas* searched and frequently seized their ships.[1] Early in 1750, for example, the Spanish seized several English, Dutch, and French vessels at Havana—after receiving positive orders there from Spain *"to trade with no Vessels whatever, but those of their own Nation."*[2] In the fall of 1750, the Spaniards seized other English vessels, took them to Havana, and condemned many of them. The authorities held the *Dispatch,* bound from Jamaica for London and taken off Porto-Purco, for fourteen weeks to await the outcome of a lawsuit. They restored the ship to her owners after first plundering her. *Guardacostas* also took two English vessels laden with logwood in the vicinity of the Bay of Honduras (the rights to cut logwood in the Bay of Campeche being in dispute between Spain and England) and condemned them at Havana. The Spanish seized and condemned too the ship of a Saint Christopher's captain who put into Havana in need of provisions *"as an Example that others for the future may not dare to put into that* Port tho' in a starving condition, which is the reason given in their proceedings."[3] A far cry from the promise of "kind entertainment" (treaty of 1670), the seizure of the Saint Christopher's galley no doubt was the result in part of the English taking advantage of this concession. However, the *South-Carolina Gazette's* conclusion was that neither the war nor the peace had put a stop to the illegal seizures and captures in the Spanish West Indies.[4]

Meanwhile the Spanish crown, still determined to end the illicit trade with her colonies, resolved to take whatever measures were necessary to prevent it. In 1751, however, the king of Spain was also anxious to maintain the peace with Great Britain. Recognizing that his own subjects were often alleged to be the principal cause of the illicit trade "so fatal to the peace," he ordered that any person in his dominions who was in the future detected in a contraband commerce with the English was to suffer death and the confiscation of all his estate and effects.[5]

Despite the strict royal orders and the severe penalties, the traffic with the English continued to thrive and was widespread in the West Indies and the rest of Spanish America including Florida. Late in 1751, for instance, a London newspaper reported that the isle and fortress of Saint Gabriel, in the Río de la Plata, had been put into the hands of Spanish troops sent there by the governor of Buenos Aires under the terms of a treaty made with Portugal. The English newspaper remarked that, "they flatter themselves that, by this step, an end will be absolutely put to the contraband trade in that part of the world."[6]

Yet, the Spanish government took all possible precautions to prevent the illicit commerce carried on by other nations with the Spanish colonies.[7] Early in 1760, for example, the king of Spain ordered his governors in Spanish America to "employ their utmost attention" to prevent all contraband trade, but to allow no act of hostility within reach of their cannon.[8] The following year (1761) a London newspaper reported that the Spanish court had new regulations for excluding all foreign nations from the South American trade.[9] Shortly before Spain officially entered the French and Indian War, she ordered (December 10, 1761) her governors in Spain and in the Spanish possessions in America to stop all English ships then in their harbors or that might enter for either protection or trade.[10] But these attempts by the Spanish crown to prevent and halt the illicit traffic with her colonies, especially that carried on by the English, were unsuccessful and only added to the deterioration and eventual breakdown of her relations with Great Britain.

The English would not give up their clandestine commerce with the Spanish colonies, but instead complained to the Spanish court about illegal searches and seizures and demanded free navigation in the West Indies. For example, Benjamin Keene, the British minister to the court of Madrid, received orders in the fall of 1750 "to make the most pressing instances"[11] to the Spanish court for the restitution of the ships and cargoes of English subjects recently seized in the West Indies and for indemnifying their proprietors for the losses sustained.[12] Keene asserted that the Spanish *guardacostas* in America not only visited all the English ships encountered there, but had seized some not involved in any contraband trade.

The Spanish king finally ordered that an inquiry be made and that his colonial governors be informed that he had no other design but the prevention of clandestine and unlawful commerce within his dominions. The governors were to conform exactly to the tenor of the treaties and the *guardacostas* were to be under instructions to do nothing that might give "any just cause for complaint."[13] Further "express" orders sent in the spring of 1751 to the governors and commanders of the Spanish colonial ports instructed them to inquire strictly into the British complaints regarding the seizures of several of their ships by Spanish *guardacostas*. If the complaints proved to be justly grounded, the ships were to be restored to their owners who were to be fully paid for the damages they suffered because of such illegal captures. The British court, in turn, instructed Keene to thank the Spanish king for the "friendly orders" he had thought proper to dispatch to his West Indian governors. Spanish governors also had instructions to be careful in the future that no English vessels be seized or retarded— unless it was certain that the captains of such vessels had contraband effects on board.[14]

In November, 1751, negotiations between Keene and the Spanish court appeared far advanced and likely to be brought to a "happy issue." The Spanish consented to the free navigation of English ships—provided they did not pass the agreed-upon limits. One of the principal obstacles blocking conclusion of the negotiations, however, was the security which the Spanish court required to ensure that the ships should not "directly or indirectly, carry on a contraband commerce."[15] This again was the crucial and fatal obstacle.

Neither the contraband trade nor the searches and seizures stopped and Anglo-Spanish relations steadily deteriorated. Late in 1751 the *"Kind Spaniards"* imprisoned for a time the crews of several English ships lost near Cuba.[16] On January 2, 1752, Spanish *guardacostas* seized the sloop *Diamond* of New York bound from Jamaica to Charleston with over six thousand dollars on board.[17] The *South-Carolina Gazette* reported that the Spanish *guardacostas* had orders to seize every English vessel that "has to the value of Ten Dollars in *Spanish* Coin on board" and observed that "Upon Complaint being made, 'tis probable we shall be told these were Pirates."[18] The *Gazette* also noted that whenever any searches or seizures were made of Dutch vessels, the Dutch governors immediately granted letters of *"Mart and Reprisal"* to the injured,

> . . . *who thereby are enabled to obtain Restitution, without going thro' the numerous Forms, and exposing themselves to as numerous Difficulties and Disappointments, that attend Complaints on Such Occasions, to the Court of Madrid.*[19]

The *Gazette,* in May, 1752, reported Keene's failure to make progress in any material part of his negotiations with the Spanish court. The minister to Spain, however, had fresh assurances that the Spanish king had sent "very precise" orders to his West Indian *guardacostas* to be more cautious in the future when visiting and taking English ships. The Spaniards assured Keene that the royal intention was to immediately release all those who were not clearly convicted or justly suspected of engaging in a contraband trade.[20]

During the summer of 1752, however, the king of Spain resolved to send a large squadron to America to support his *guardacostas* in preventing "every kind" of contraband traffic. Ferdinand VI's resolution followed information that the British court intended to sent a squadron to the West Indies to protect British commerce and navigation.[21] But this same year the Spanish king sent "positive orders" to the Havana governor to pay from the royal treasury the indemnification agreed upon for the English ships illegally taken by the *guardacostas.* There were again warnings to the Spanish colonial governors to be more careful in the future to prevent like causes of complaint.[22] Ferdinand VI also ordered his American governors to pay the proprietors of English ships which had been taken since the cessation of hostilities their full value.[23]

Reports from Madrid in September, 1753, however, insinuated that the differences over navigation of the English in the West Indies and the contraband trade with the Spanish colonies would be determined in a few months. Ferdinand VI, it seems, intended to send such a reinforcement to his American *guarda-costas* that the dispute must "needs be brought to an issue some way or other."[24] Late that same year, London received fresh complaints from Jamaica and other West Indian colonies of Spanish *guardacostas* seizing several vessels without "any lawful reason whatsoever," according to the English colonists.[25]

The Anglo-Spanish differences over trade and navigation in America again proved to be irreconcilable. The British continued to demand from Spain free navigation in the West Indies without search or visit;[26] while a primary object of the Spanish ministry was to maintain a formidable naval force in America to support the "honor" of the Spanish crown and to protect Spanish commerce which continued to be "clandestinely invaded by interlopers."[27] The British demanded free navigation and an end to search and seizure, but were quite unwilling to give up their profitable trade with the Spanish colonies. Spain, determined to prevent the illicit traffic, thus continued to search and oftentimes seize British ships.

By early 1755 the long-talked-of treaty for regulating the commerce of the British in the American waters was no longer the subject of conversation at Madrid. Instead, a treaty of mutual assistance with France, in case of insult by the English marine, was the center of public attention. Both the Spanish and French courts were anxious to confine the English to their existing limits in America, since the increasing power of their colonies was already formidable and had aroused jealousy,[28] and, of course, threatened the small Spanish colony in Florida. France also attempted to persuade Spain to make common cause against England in America since the Spanish suffered so "terribly" from the contraband trade in that part of the world. The French indicated their willingness to cooperate in ending such practices by any nation whatsoever.[29] When war finally did break out in America between the French and English in 1756, Spain maintained an uneasy neutrality until 1762.

Trade in the Southeast
1748-1762

In the Southeast a steady and flourishing trade began once again between the English colonies and Spanish Florida soon after the War of Jenkins' Ear. Saint Augustine apparently first learned of the peace from an English ship which departed Charleston for the Spanish port in September, 1748, soon after the English themselves received the news.[30] Approximately five ships sailed from Charleston to Saint Augustine during the last four months of 1748.[31] English merchants at Charleston, Savannah, and New York were apparently eager to resume their trade with the Floridians. In 1749, for example, a total of eleven English ships sailed from Charleston to Saint Augustine, and an additional six to Havana.[32] In 1750, the year Havana received the Spanish orders that the colonies were to trade with no nation but their own, nine vessels sailed from Charleston to Saint Augustine; although none apparently sailed from Charleston for Havana that year.[33] The number of English ships plying the waters between Charleston and Saint Augustine was greatest in 1749 and 1750—possibly because of the need of the Florida colony for supplies after the hardships and privations of the recent war. Thereafter, the traffic with Spanish Florida continued steadily until the declaration of war between Great Britain and Spain in 1762, although the number of ships carrying provisions from Charleston to Saint Augustine apparently ranged from two or three a year to as many as seven or more.[34] Both South Carolina and Georgia, however, oftentimes shipped supplies, such as cattle, overland to Saint Augustine.

Merchants in Charleston traded not only with Saint Augustine but also with Havana. In 1756 an unusual number of Spanish ships called at Charleston on voyages to and from Cuba. Other Spanish vessels—place of origin and destination not recorded—also put in at Charleston, although several of these were ships in distress. Since the traffic with both Saint Augustine and Havana usually employed English ships, it is not certain whether or not all of the above Spanish vessels actually engaged in any trade with the English colony. The vessels from Cuba, however, apparently enjoyed an illicit tobacco trade with Charleston.[35]

English ships sailed, too, from Charleston to Cádiz and Seville in Spain.[36] So it would appear that Spain took advantage of the opportunity to trade with England's colonies during the same period she was trying to prevent the traffic between the English and her own colonies. For South Carolina had a license for many years to ship rice directly to the southward of Cape Finisterre in northwestern Spain.[37]

In September, 1759, two Spanish schooners arrived in Savannah, Georgia, from Havana and another from Saint Augustine. Again it is not certain whether or not they were there to trade or had some other purpose.[38] However, English merchants usually took advantage of all opportunities to trade.

The illicit trade in the Southeast benefited both the English and Spanish colonists. It enabled the Spaniards at Saint Augustine to obtain much-needed supplies and eventually even the Spanish government recognized the advantages of the commerce. Here—in direct contrast to the strict Spanish trade restrictions—the Spanish crown seemingly sanctioned a certain amount of traffic with the English colonies in order to supply its Florida colony.

Prior to the peace in 1748, Governor Manuel de Montiano (1746) openly urged free trade with the English colonies to end the miserable conditions in Florida. Montiano was aware of the strict Spanish laws against trade with the English or any other foreign colonies. But he was also aware of the advantages to be gained from such a trade[39]—especially since there was in fact trade with the English colonies off and on at least as far back as 1717. English goods were of high quality, their prices were lower, and there were no risks in transportation.

Montiano's advice was not futile. For a number of years later the Havana Company, faced with the responsibility of supplying the Florida colony, began making contracts *(asientos)* with English merchants in New York and Charleston. The company's officials, however, had permission from the Florida governor and council *(Junta)* and the Spanish crown to purchase supplies for Florida elsewhere if not available in Cuba. Thus, after 1750, complaints from Florida governors of privation and misery due to lack of supplies decreased. The governor was assured of receiving a regular supply of good merchandise at a low cost. The supply problems further lessened in this period since the subsidy to pay for the English supplies apparently arrived in Cuba without the delays so often experienced in the past.[40]

Letters to Ferdinand VI from the Florida governor in July, 1752, and August, 1756, told of English ships from New York and South Carolina arriving in Saint Augustine with supplies contracted for by the Havana Company,[41] so that the Spanish crown definitely was aware of the fact that the Havana Company was taking advantage of its privilege to trade with the English colonies.

Although the Spanish crown seemingly sanctioned the arrangements of the Havana Company with English merchants at Charleston and New York, this apparently did not give any English vessel the right to trade at Saint Augustine. In 1753 the governor of Florida took steps against a South Carolinian captain because a passenger on his ship sold goods illicitly in Saint Augustine. Governor Alonso Fernández de Heredia in 1756 exposed the Cuban seamen involved in the illicit traffic with South Carolina since they were selling goods obtained in that English colony in Saint Augustine.[42] Such measures were unusual, however, because Saint Augustine generally welcomed any source of supply—especially when the colony was in extreme want.

The Southeastern English colonists—eager to resume and expand trade with Spanish Florida after the war—apparently took full advantage of the opportunity to supply the Florida garrison on a more legitimate basis. In South Carolina, for instance, this traffic was an important factor in the economy. Governor James Glen, in a speech to the general asssembly of South Carolina in March, 1749, had only good news—the best news being the signing of the definitive peace treaty in October, 1748.[43] South Carolina's economic outlook in the spring of 1749 appeared bright to the governor. Rice, which for several years during the war had sold for ten to twenty shillings currency per hundred weight, now sold for fifty-five shillings and three pounds currency per hundred weight.[44] Many markets, closed during the war, were again open. Saint Augustine, for example, probably received some rice from Charleston, since rice was a major crop of South Carolina. Gold and silver received from Havana and Saint Augustine in exchange for rice, beef, pork, and other goods contributed considerably to the South Carolina economy. This gold and silver apparently did not remain long in South Carolina, but was shipped in part to the northern colonies in exchange for their goods with a larger part going to Great Britain to "help out" the South Carolina remittances.[45]

Glen was eager, however, to expand the colony's economy. Speaking to both houses of the assembly in November, 1749, the Carolina governor observed that in a time of war it was discouraging and difficult to attempt and succeed in any plan of improvement. But, he urged, since all was finally "calm and serene," that South Carolinians "employ the present Peace, Plenty, and Felicity that God blesses us with in improving the Country, and fixing, as far as human Prudence can reach, its future Happiness."[46] The governor suggested ways to accomplish this goal. Since attempts to cultivate indigo in South Carolina had not been too successful, the governor thought that it might be advisable to give "suitable encouragement" to a person from either the French or Spanish settlements to settle in South Carolina.[47] Among other items Glen also pointed out that South Carolina abounded in cattle and lay ". . . commodiously to the Sugar Colonies and foreign Settlements for a Market."[48]

Thus the trade between Charleston and Saint Augustine once again thrived as did the trade between New York and Saint Augustine. Charleston merchants in September, 1752, for example, received a quantity of money from Havana on their "Accompt" (account).[49] Floridians again imported and exported goods to the English colonies. On March 26, 1753, for instance, the *Elizabeth* (Charles Reid) set sail from Charleston for Saint Augustine with a cargo of flour, beer, bread, butter, grindstones, beeswax, and axes.[50] The *Saint Augustine* of New York (Richard Wright) returned on October 13, 1753, from a voyage to Saint Augustine with ten thousand feet of plank; while the *Lark* of New York (William Hyer) returned to New York on July 3, 1754, from the Spanish colony with a cargo of seventeen sea tortoises.[51]

However, intercolonial affairs did not remain "calm and serene." The war brewing between the French and English colonists eventually curtailed and finally stopped the English traffic with Saint Augustine. For after the French and Indian

55

War began in 1756, the Board of Trade in England instructed its colonial governors to take steps to prevent the exporting of supplies to the French.[52]

Consequently, the governor of New York, Sir Charles Hardy, on December 29, 1756, laid an embargo on that port aimed at preventing the exportation of provisions to neutral powers and from them frequently to the French. There were, however, immediate objections to the embargo in the case of trade with Saint Augustine.[53] William Walton, a merchant of New York City, pleaded in a memorial to Governor Hardy in January, 1757, that an "express Exception" ought to be made in favor of the Florida colony.[54] The colony, Walton stated, was in "eminent Danger" of perishing as a result of its dependence upon him for its "daily Subsistance."[55] For Saint Augustine he claimed—either through ignorance or self-interest—had "no Intercourse with the other British colonies."[56]

Walton took special care to emphasize that the small Spanish garrison was under strict orders not to contract with him for more supplies than were necessary for its own use. So, according to him, there was no chance at all that the Floridians would ever succor the French with provisions obtained from the English.[57] The merchant swore—as did Charles Hicks, one of his former agents at Saint Augustine, and William Hyer, a sailor in his employ—that there was in fact a cédula containing "an absolute Prohibition" against re-transporting provisions from the Florida port to any other port whether foreign or Spanish.[58]

To further strengthen his case, Walton pointed out to the New York governor the "Advantages" that the province of New York gained from the trade with Saint Augustine. Since the exports to the Spanish colony consisted of the staples of New York this, the merchant felt, gave "Very great Incouragement" to New Yorkers in their "Manufactories and Produce." On the other hand, the silver received from Saint Augustine in return contributed in a "singular Manner, to the Support of the Credit of our Paper Emissions."[59] Walton added too that if the authorities did not make an exception in favor of his contract to supply the Floridians it would be "very injurious" to himself. For the merchant had a contract with the Royal Company of the

Island of Cuba (Havana Company) formulated shortly after the Peace of Aix-la-Chapelle. In fact, Walton's family had had similar contracts for supplying the Spanish garrison as far back as 1726. In this instance the merchant-memorialist stood to lose some sixty thousand "Mill'd Dollars" in arrears due to him—plus two vessels laden with provisions waiting only for permission to sail.[60] However, Walton took care to assure the governor that he was not in any way seeking a disguise to serve his own interests at the expense of his country. He had no "Sinister Views."[61] Still, he did not wish to lose a valuable contract.

The plea of the New York merchant apparently was not unheeded—nor was his pocketbook injured too greatly. On August 9, 1757, the king and council at Whitehall took the prohibition off the exportation of corn, grain, and other goods from the province of New York to the garrison at Saint Augustine. The goods thus exported were to be for "Supporting the Garrison there" only. Security in "treble" was to be given so that goods "designed" for the Florida colony would not be landed or sold elsewhere.[62]

Charleston merchants also kept on trading with the garrison at Saint Augustine in spite of wartime restrictions intended to prevent any English goods from reaching the enemy. William Henry Lyttelton, the governor of South Carolina, issued a proclamation in October, 1756, strictly forbidding the export of any provisions from any port of South Carolina excepting rice on vessels bound to Europe.[63] But Lyttelton found it necessary to issue another proclamation in November, 1756, revoking and making void his proclamation of October 25 in so far as it extended or could be construed to extend to the restraining of exports to any of the British dominions.[64] Then, early in 1757, the governor issued a proclamation specifically aimed at preventing the English trade to the French Islands and colonies carried on through Dutch and other neutral powers[65]—including the Spanish. Saint Augustine, however, was again an exception, since South Carolina's trade with Spanish Florida continued. Several ships sailed to Saint Augustine from Charleston later in the same year[66] and additional supplies went overland. Enterprising South Carolinians, for example, drove four hundred head of cattle overland from Charleston to Saint Augustine in June, 1757. While there the South Carolinians made contracts for supplying the Floridians with "many more large Gangs."[67]

Thus the *South-Carolina Gazette* complained the same month that the cattle driven to Saint Augustine in the previous nine months "incredibly" exceeded the quantity that the Spanish garrison could possibly consume. The *Gazette* noted, too, that it was extremely difficult for butchers to supply the Charleston market,

> . . . and that too with very ordinary Beef. Is it not hence to be feared, that St. Augustine is converting into a Magazine for certain Purposes? And ought not we to guard against the Possibility of its being made so? [68]

But it was the Georgians who took action at this time. In July, 1757, there were reports from Georgia that the Spaniards at Saint Augustine were "laying in great Stores of all Kinds of Provisions."[69] In order to prevent the Florida colony from becoming a channel of supply to the enemies of Great Britain, the Georgia assembly resolved to put an end to the driving of cattle overland from South Carolina to Florida by means of an act which would subject all cattle or provisions driven or conveyed to the south of Ogeachy to seizure.[70] Although Charleston received word later the same month that the Georgia assembly had actually passed the necessary legislation to restrain the carrying of provisions to Saint Augustine without a license,[71] it does not appear that South Carolina passed any similar legislation. Yet it seems rather ironic that later in the same year the governor of Georgia interposed in a dispute between the Occoni Indians and the Spaniards at Saint Augustine with the result that the dispute was "happily accommodated" and some captive Spaniards released.[72]

The year 1758 is possibly the only year prior to the formal declaration of war between Great Britain and Spain in which no ships sailed from Charleston to Saint Augustine. But an embargo on all shipping was in effect from April to the beginning of August.[73] After the lifting of this embargo, however, reports in the *South-Carolina Gazette* "confidently assert-

58

English Colonial Ports
Involved in Trade with
Spanish Florida in
the Mid-18th Century

ed" that an effective stop would soon be put to the sending of provisions to Saint Augustine from South Carolina and Georgia and also from New York and other British "plantations." Saint Augustine, it seems, was an "Asylum and Rendezvous" for French privateers and thus a threat to the British colonies in a time of war.[74]

Still the English vacillated in their policy toward the Floridians. The British ship *Zephyr* in the fall of 1758, for example, seized a schooner she caught clandestinely carrying provisions to Saint Augustine.[75] Then, late in 1758, the general assembly of Georgia passed additional legislation to prevent provisions being sent by land or water to the Florida garrison —under severe penalties—without a license from the governor. Yet the Georgia assembly did not intend to stop all trade with Saint Augustine, but *"to restrain any more being sent there than may be necessary for the Subsistance of the* Spaniards *themselves"* and thereby, if possible, prevent them from supplying French privateers.[76] Moreover, the following year the *Gazette* spoke kindly of the neighboring subjects of its "good ally" the king of Spain;[77] while several English vessels sailed from Charleston for the nearby Florida colony,[78] among them the *Scriven* (Thomas Tucker) with "Sundry goods per certificate."[79]

Hence, Spanish Florida obtained a certain amount of supplies from the English colonies until the closing stages of the French and Indian War despite the fact that the Floridians succored French privateers. The trade was not stopped at this time contrary to assertions that it would be. For English vessels still called at Saint Augustine in 1760. The sloop *Cornelia* (Jonathan Lawrence) left the port of Hampton, Virginia, on April 17, 1760, for the Spanish colony with a cargo of lard, beef, salt, and fifty-three "Iron Potts";[80] while the *Speedwell* (William Rogers) departed Charleston on September 18, 1760, for Saint Augustine with "Sundry Brittish goods."[81] The *Cornelia* and *Speedwell* were only two of the English vessels to visit the Spanish outpost during this year.

But Georgia in June of the same year again attempted to curb the trade with the Spaniards in Florida. Governor Henry Ellis and his council in a June 17 meeting resolved to issue a proclamation to prohibit vessels sailing from that province to Saint Augustine or any port of the Spanish or French dominions on the north side of the Bay of Mexico.[82] This time there was no mention of merely "restraining" supplies. Although the proclamation did not specifically prohibit overland trade, it required a license from the governor who also had the authority to block that means of supply.

Nevertheless, in July, 1760, Governor Ellis again met with his council in Savannah—this time to discuss the expediency of supplying "ye Spanish" with provisions. Ellis informed the council members that he had information that the Spaniards in Saint Augustine were greatly in want of fresh provisions. In fact, so great was their want that to obtain supplies for the Florida colony, Governor Lucas Fernando de Palacio y Valenzuela had written and promised the Georgia governor that he would maintain a "friendly Correspondence" with the English, restore all slaves thereafter who fled from Georgia to Florida, and no longer allow French privateers to take shelter in the harbor at Saint Augustine. Ellis pointed out that other English colonies still enjoyed the privilege of supplying the Spaniards. The governor also reminded his council that the law recently passed in Georgia to prevent the enemy from being supplied with provisions reserved to him a discretionary power to grant licenses for supplying provisions to the Spaniards for their own use. The governor then inquired of the council whether granting a license to some "proper Person or Persons" who were willing to supply the Florida garrison with a certain number of cattle "might not be expedient." The council upon consideration recommended that to

... *grant the Spaniards a present Supply not exceeding three hundred Head of black Cattle might not only be proper but answer some very good Purposes at this Juncture.*[83]

Palacio's personal plea to his neighboring governor apparently netted him a supply of beef for his garrison. Moreover, the Floridians continued to obtain goods from the nearby English. In August, 1761, South Carolinians cleared two vessels at Charleston for voyages to Saint Augustine, presumably loaded with supplies for the Spanish colony.[84] Unfortunately for the

Spaniards at Saint Augustine, however, there was a formal declaration of war between Great Britain and Spain in January, 1762, and once again the supply problem of the Florida colony grew desperate.

Yet the English and Spanish merchants at both Havana and Saint Augustine early in February, 1762, did not appear to have even the least apprehension of a rupture between their respective countries—despite the fact that there were then in the harbor of Havana fifteen Spanish ships of the line, four frigates, and a sloop all ready to put to sea. Havana had two other ships of the line recently launched there and daily expected six more from Spain. In addition there were recently arrived troops at Havana—apparently destined to reinforce the garrisons at Pensacola and Saint Augustine.[85] No doubt reluctant to end their profitable trade, the merchants, therefore, were not too anxious to inquire about an impending war.

But Governor James Wright of Georgia in a council meeting held in May, 1762, presented the declaration of war against Spain and the orders for proclaiming it in Georgia in order that the British subjects in that province could do their duty "to distress and annoy the Subjects of Spain."[86] Wright had orders to be vigorous and severe in preventing provisions being sent to Saint Augustine.[87] Therefore in the proclamation of war issued May 25, 1762, he forbade any trade with the subjects of the king of Spain and warned that anyone found engaging in such activities would be "rigorously and severely prosecuted."[88]

Governor Wright proved to be a man of his word. At a council meeting two days after his proclamation, he informed the council members that one Samuel Piles had been brought in on suspicion of "holding Correspondence" with the enemy at Saint Augustine and of trying to arrange a peace between the Spanish and Creek Indians, the latter being then at peace with the English and at war with the Spanish. Upon examination Piles said that he had gone to Saint Augustine about six weeks before and had taken with him 170 bushels of corn and "Pease" and 100 shoats, but had heard nothing then of a war being declared between Spain and England—although he heard about it while there.

At Saint Augustine, Piles also learned that about four thousand dollars were owed to him there and applied about it to the governor who assured him that he should not lose his money but that he would have to return again with another cargo before he could receive it. Piles stated that he then told the governor that he could not return if war had been declared between their respective countries. Whereupon Piles said he returned to Frederica and made the "strictest Inquiry" and could not discover that war had been declared there or in any other part of Georgia or in South Carolina. Therefore he made preparations to go with another cargo to Saint Augustine consisting of shingles, boards, some dry goods, and about thirty shoats. Piles also denied the charges that he had attempted to patch up a quarrel between the Spanish and Creek Indians. He claimed that he had been asked to do so about eighteen months previously by a sergeant major at Saint Augustine, but had refused to do so even if he could because he knew he might be tried for life if the governors of Georgia or Carolina found out about it.

However, in a deposition given by Benjamin Wilson against Piles, Wilson testified that he had heard Piles say that he would try and make peace between the Creeks and Spanish. The governor and council felt that Piles' actions were possibly of "dangerous consequences" to the peace and safety of Georgia. Consequently, they placed him under bond for good behavior, and eventually referred his case to the attorney general for appropriate action.[89] Poor Piles also was apparently not too anxious to find out about the war—at least until he got his money.

Both Georgia and South Carolina took additional steps this same spring to prevent any trade being carried on with the Spaniards at Saint Augustine. Georgia, for example, made Sunbury a port of entry and appointed "proper" officers to serve there.[90] South Carolina passed an act in May, 1762, to regulate the coasting trade and to prevent illicit trade with the enemy. Governor Thomas Boone noted that despite the acts of Parliament designed to regulate the trade; British subjects nevertheless supplied his majesty's enemies with provisions, ammunition, and stores. The act therefore empowered the governor to appoint officers to prevent such abuses.[91]

Thus the declaration of war between Great Britain and Spain brought a virtual halt to the previously steady flow of trade between the English and Spaniards in the Southeast. After Spain entered the French and Indian War, the English seemingly made every effort to prevent any illicit trade with the Floridians. Yet some still existed. In the summer of 1762, for example, Georgia sent a scout boat to seize a vessel reportedly taking on a cargo of hogs and other provisions at Talbot Island near the San Juan River and destined for Saint Augustine.[92] But the deterioration of conditions in the Florida garrison indicate that the British measures were, in the final stages of this last intercolonial war, generally successful. For want of supplies compelled the Spaniards at Saint Augustine—as in the War of Jenkins' Ear—to resort to privateering in order to survive.

Privateering in the Southeast During the French and Indian War

In the French and Indian War, privateering once again flourished in the Southeastern waters and in the rest of America, the West Indies, and Europe. Even though Spain was neutral until January, 1762, both she and her American colonies actively supplied the French in America. For example, Spanish vessels and/or vessels under Spanish colors carried provisions to the French in Canada,[93] in the West Indies, and in other parts of the New World. French privateers from the West Indies and Mississippi oftentimes obtained provisions and even fitted out from Spanish colonial ports, such as Havana and Saint Augustine, to prey on English shipping.

Prior to Spain's entry into the war, the resulting intercolonial relationships in the Southeast were a bit unusual. The illicit—though seemingly sanctioned—trade between the English colonies and Spanish Florida of course continued. After the war between the French and English colonists began, however, part of the supplies received in Saint Augustine from the English colonies apparently provisioned French privateers which then sailed from the Florida colony to ply the coasts of the same English colonies and prey on their shipping. On one occasion, in the summer of 1760, a French privateer seized an English vessel bound from New York for Saint Augustine presumably with supplies for the Spanish garrison.[94]

The Spaniards in both Florida and the West Indies first began to aid the French shortly after the outbreak of hostilities in 1756. Not only did the Spaniards at Saint Augustine oftentimes provision the French, but, in addition, the authorities apparently allowed individual Spaniards to aid the French cause in other ways. Don Julian de la Vega of Saint Augustine, who was well known and remembered by the Southeastern English colonists for his success in making prizes of their vessels during the previous war, became the commander of a French privateer. The Spanish privateersman had "engaged" to ply the Southeastern English coasts in order to supply the French Islands and Mississippi "with as much Provisions as they may want."[95] Other Spaniards belonged to the crews of the French privateers plying in the Southeastern waters. Charleston in 1757, for example, took into custody three Spaniards on suspicion of belonging to French privateers and of coming to South Carolina to obtain intelligence.[96]

Furthermore, French ships from Europe often escaped the British men-of-war and privateers in America by putting into Spanish ports and producing fraudulent clearances and/or pretending to be Spanish or Dutch.[97] In the summer of 1759 the *South-Carolina Gazette* reported that most of the vessels then trading for France wore Spanish colors and thus hoped to avoid strict examination by the British men-of-war and privateers. The French, incidentally, were not the only ones who sailed under false colors. English smugglers who made use of the port of Monte Christi (Cristi) in Santo Domingo (Española) were not above "borrowing" the papers of Spanish vessels lying there, and then proceeding to Port-au-Prince, or some other French port where they sold their cargoes and purchased sugar, rum, etc., having of course given security to restore the "borrowed" papers on their return to Monte Christi.[98]

Harassed by the French privateers, the English colonists in the Southeast naturally resented the aid the French received at Saint Augustine. But, although the English threatened to halt all trade to Spanish Florida, they merely curtailed it prior to 1762. The Spaniards in the Florida garrison, on the other hand, promised only when the occasion or necessity demanded it to stop aiding the French. The British no doubt felt that it was expedient to keep the Spaniards out of the war as long as possible and willingly supplied the needs of the Floridians themselves. The Spaniards at Saint Augustine, whose interests naturally lay more with the French due to Spain's disputes with Great Britain took full advantage of the situation. The Florida colony sought and obtained supplies from the English colonies and yet aided the French—ironically with English goods—in order to impair the British cause. Saint Augustine played a shrewd game but she struck out in 1762.

Compelled once again to fit out privateers in order to protect their own trade, the English colonists in the Southeast began this task early in the war. Charleston "at last" fitted out a privateer in January, 1757, which it seems was not soon enough in the opinion of the *South-Carolina Gazette*.[99] By May of the same year at least one additional privateer was also fitted out from Charleston,[100] while the province of Georgia later fitted out the privateer *George*.[101]

In the meantime, however, the British government sent a circular (Whitehall, May 20, 1757) to all its governors in North America informing them of the "Pyratical Behaviour" of several privateers fitted out in North America toward the Spanish in the West Indies, especially the *Peggy* of New York and a privateer from Halifax. George II had received with "greatest Indignation" an "Account of Proceedings, on the Part of His Subjects, not only contrary to all Humanity, and Good Faith" but also contrary to the general instructions given to privateers and a direct breach of an additional one of the previous October regarding Spanish vessels. Consequently, George II directed the governors of New York and Nova Scotia to begin prosecution against the owners, masters, and securities of the two-accused privateers. The king further ordered all his colonial governors to acquaint all privateersmen with the above instructions and to warn them that the "severest" prosecutions would be taken against those who acted contrary to the instructions and thus threatened the harmony which George II

65

was then desirous to preserve with the Spanish crown.[102]

Meanwhile, the governor of Cuba during the summer of 1757 sent three xebecks (small three-masted ships) to search for the English privateers that had lately committed "outrages" on some Spanish vessels. The Spanish xebecks were to force all the English privateers they met into Havana so that the instigator of the "outrages" could be discovered. The Cuban governor also sent an additional vessel to probe all the northern colonial ports of Great Britain.[103] These British "outrages," perhaps, grew out of the fact that the Spanish gave aid to the French.

The *South-Carolina Gazette* reported in June, 1757, that there was a possibility that the court of Spain might break with Great Britain.[104] In order to halt the transportation of troops etc. to and from Mississippi and an illicit trade there, the British ordered men-of-war from the Jamaica station to cruise through the Windward passage, the "Old-Straights of Bahama," off the west end of the Bahama Bank, and then into the "Bay of Mexico" off "Mississippi," and thus back to Jamaica. An additional squadron was to be stationed at Port Royal, South Carolina, where the cruisers could be on the track of French ships coming through the Gulf, which was the route of all the vessels from Louisiana and many from Santo Domingo. In the event of war with Spain, the British squadron would have the double advantage of being in the track of all the homeward-bound Spanish galleons and flota.[105]

Meanwhile, French privateers—"victualled" at Saint Augustine—still infested the Southeastern waters. Three French privateers, all supplied from Saint Augustine, plied the Georgia coast in August, 1757.[106] In June, 1758, French privateers still sailed from and returned to Saint Augustine with their English prizes. But the Florida governor seemingly had been warned or foresaw that the English might cut off their trade with Florida if he continued to allow the French to use the harbor at Saint Augustine as a rendezvous for their privateers. Early in the summer, therefore, he apparently found it expedient to discourage the French, at least for a while, and so ordered out a French privateer along with her four prizes.[107] In July of the same year, however, there were three French privateers, all small and ill manned, cruising between Cape Fear and Frederica; while the *True Blue* privateer, previously of Charleston, was being fitted out as a fourth at Saint Augustine. Reports from Georgia indicated that the French privateer which had recently engaged their province sloop "was uncommonly well fitted and manned from *St. Augustine* for that Purpose."[108] Consequently, the Georgians intended to ask the Lords of Admiralty to station a man-of-war there for their protection and "Real Service."[109]

In 1756, only one French privateer ventured so far as South Carolina; in 1757, two; and then in 1758, at least four. The *South-Carolina Gazette* urged that action be taken to prevent the French privateers from swarming on the coasts and doing *"incredible Mischief"* and observed that "St. Augustine, *in that Case will be as hurtful to our Trade now, as it was in the last War."*[110]

For in August, 1758, two French privateers fitted out from Saint Augustine cruised off Georgia; while two more prepared to sail from the Florida garrison.[111] A French privateer in the fall of the year called at the Florida port on her way to "Mississippi" with her eleven prizes.[112] However, in March, 1759, Charleston received word that no French privateers would in the future "receive any Countenance at *St. Augustine*."[113]

The Floridians attempted at times to convince the Carolinians of their good faith. The sloops *Lark* and *Cornelia*, for example, arrived in Charleston in August, 1761, with news that the French privateer which had seized some Negroes at Tybee had been at Saint Augustine, but was "immediately ordered away by the Governor."[114] This was, perhaps, again mere expediency on the part of the Florida governor because the English vessels had apparently brought supplies to the Florida garrison. Since shortly after their return to Charleston with the news of the Florida governor's actions, the *Lark* and *Cornelia* again sailed for Saint Augustine presumably with more supplies.

The inevitable rupture occurred in January, 1762, with a formal declaration of war between the courts of Spain and Great Britain. Both Charles III and George III issued orders to their respective subjects prohibiting trade between the Spanish and English. The two monarchs also gave orders for granting commissions (letters of marque and reprisal) to fit out privateers to cruise against the vessels of the other.[115] The king of Spain, in addition, relinquished his share of all prizes (twenty per cent) in order to encourage his subjects to fit out privateers.[116] However, the subjects of Charles III at Saint Augustine actually needed no such encouragement. For once their trade with the English colonies ended, the Floridians turned to their privateers to supply the Florida colony. Privateering therefore increased in the Southeastern waters after 1762—because the English had both the French and Spanish to contend with until the end of the war.

Spanish and English privateers were also active in the West Indies and in the rest of America after 1762. Early in the spring of 1762, eight small privateers were ready to sail from Havana to cruise off the coast of America as soon as there was a proclamation of war against Great Britain.[117] The British West Indian Islands for their part fitted out about forty-five privateers to cruise against the Spaniards.[118] The Bay of Mexico, for example, swarmed with the English privateers.[119]

Hence, Charleston in April, 1762, busily fitted out privateers. The schooners *Major Rogers* and *Harlequin,* once outfitted, would carry 50 and 70 men respectively; while the *Charles-Town* was also being fitted out with the "greatest expedition." This latter vessel was a fine brigantine (a two-masted ship) which mounted 14 double-fortified six pounders and 20 swivel guns and would carry 120 men. The Carolinians encouraged volunteers to serve on their privateers and talked of outfitting more from Charleston if some vessels based there but then at sea returned safely from their voyages.[120] These privateers sent out from Charleston were not without success. The *Major Rogers* returned in May, 1762, with a French sloop, *le St: Ferdinand,* captured en route from New Orleans to Saint Augustine with a cargo of furs; while the *Harlequin* during the same month plied the waters off the port of Saint Augustine.[121]

English privateers in the West Indies were no less successful. This same spring they took several rich Spanish vessels—some loaded with cocoa—and carried them into St. Christopher's. English privateers also carried other prizes into Martinique,[122] the latter port having been captured by the British. Meanwhile

68

at Havana, the Spanish outfitted two Spanish galleys in May, 1762, to scour the coast from Cape Romain to Cape Florida.[123] At Saint Augustine this same month a quarter-galley of two carriage guns and forty-five men, most of whom were French, cruised off the bar of Saint Augustine, seemingly to give notice of any approaching enemy; but no privateers were then fitting out from the Florida garrison.[124]

By July, 1762, there were indications that the Spaniards in Saint Augustine had not recently "received any supplies"[125] because the English were successful in blocking both the French and Spanish supply lines. The measures taken by General Jeffery Amherst, the commander in chief of the British forces in America, to prevent exportation of provisions etc. from the northern colonies had very favorable results—for the English. At Española and other places, the French were in such straits that they could barely subsist themselves and were practically unable to fit out even their own merchantmen, much less whole fleets of privateers as previously. The English expected that these measures, aided by the stoppage of trade in the Southeast no doubt, would also contribute to an easier and earlier reduction of Havana, "if it should be conquered." The British felt too that this would impair the Florida colony and would "certainly have prevented our trade being annoyed by privateers from St. Augustine, had orders been received there in due time to grant commissions."[126]

The British forces took Moro Castle, which guarded the entrance to Havana, by storm on July 30, 1762. On August 12 the city of Havana with all its dependencies, and all the Spanish ships in the harbor, surrendered by capitulation.[127] Charles III— extremely shocked and most upset when he heard that Cuba was lost—would see no one for four days afterward and threatened vengeance on his ministers who had "imposed on him, by assuring him the place was impregnable."[128]

The governor of South Carolina, by contrast, received a letter from the Earl of Albemarle dated Havana, August 27, 1762, in which Albemarle told of the "happy success" of the British arms in the West Indies (Cuba being considered the key to the West Indies) and pointed out that:

In the general satisfaction this event must give to all his majesty's subjects, I flatter myself the province of South Carolina will take a particular part, as they can have little to fear from St. Augustine for the future, whom this conquest has deprived of every resource by which the Spaniards might be enabled to annoy or disturb your government.[129]

Albemarle underestimated the Spaniards in Florida. Saint Augustine was, certainly, in the most critical straits by the summer of 1762 with the stoppage of all supplies from the British colonies and then, in addition, from Havana. It was, however, after the loss of Cuba that Saint Augustine became active in fitting out privateers. Deprived of every other resource, the Floridians became dependent on their privateersmen for their very survival. After the conquest of Cuba, Spaniards from Saint Augustine plied the English coasts along with their French allies in increasing numbers and contrary to Albemarle's prediction greatly disturbed and annoyed the English colonies.

The Spanish privateers impelled by deteriorating conditions in Saint Augustine were not without success. In September, 1762, the *San Christoval*, a small Spanish xebeque of only five guns—one of which was cracked—and about sixty men went privateering in the Southeastern waters under the command of Don Martino. Early on September 5, the Spanish privateer captured off the bar of Charleston the *Palacre James* bound from New Providence for Charleston with a cargo of rice, lignum vitae, and sugar, and immediately sent her to Saint Augustine. On the thirteenth of September the *San Christoval* took the *Success* of Rhode Island en route from Georgia to Rhode Island with a cargo of rice and naval stores. Two days later she took the *Anne* of Charleston en route from Georgia to her home port with a cargo of rice and seven Negroes. The Spaniards got about 70 barrels of rice in the *Palacre James*, 60 in the *Success,* and 121 in the *Anne,* any of which cargoes must have been "a very seasonable supply to the garrison of St. Augustine, almost starving when the privateer came out."[130] Disturbed and annoyed by the activities of its Spanish neighbors, the *South-Carolina Gazette* felt that it should not be too difficult "especially now the Havana is ours, to starve the garrison of St. Augustine, or oblige them to surrender, by two frigates from this port alternately blocking up that port."[131]

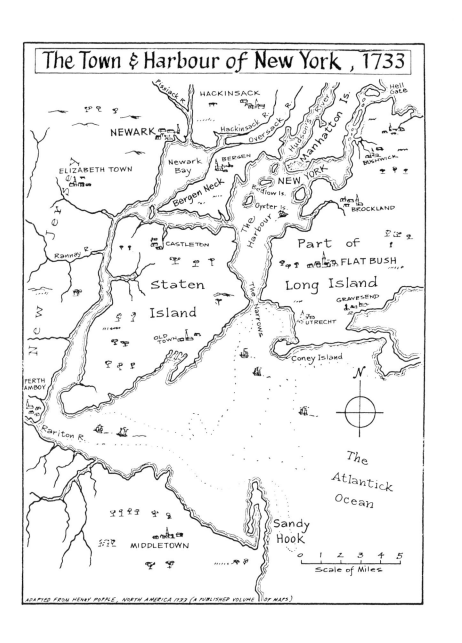

The Town & Harbour of New York, 1733

Pissaick R.
HACKINSACK
Hackinsack R.
Oversack R.
Hudson's River
Manhattan Is.
Hell Gate
NEWARK
BUSHWICK
Newark Bay
BERGEN
ELIZABETH TOWN
Bergen Neck
NEW YORK
Bedlow Is.
BROCKLAND
Oyster Is.
The Harbour
Rannay R.
CASTLETON
Part of
FLAT BUSH
N   e   w   J   e   r
Staten
Island
Long Island
GRAVESEND
The Narrows
UTRECHT
OLD TOWN
PERTH AMBOY
Coney Island
Rariton R.
N
The
Atlantick
Ocean
Sandy Hook
MIDDLETOWN

0   1   2   3   4   5
Scale of Miles

ADAPTED FROM HENRY POPPLE, NORTH AMERICA 1733 (A PUBLISHED VOLUME OF MAPS)

The Spanish and French privateering continued, however. In October two small privateers, one a French sloop and the other a Spanish schooner, prepared to sail from Saint Augustine.[132] The same month a persistent Spanish privateer chased a vessel from Rhode Island for a whole day off Cape Hatteras.[133]

Spanish privateersmen—emboldened and spurred on by the plight of the garrison at Saint Augustine—persisted despite the fact that the English colonists, in addition to their own privateers, had the services of at least four British men-of-war, the *Bonetta, Mercury, Success,* and *Epreuve,* all of which were stationed in the Southeastern waters to protect British shipping.[134] The *South-Carolina Gazette* related in December, 1762, the exploits of a Spanish privateer from Saint Augustine that had "the hardiness to infest our coast, even while two of his majesty's ships are out upon a cruize in quest of her."[135]

A new sloop, New England built, but with only eight carriage guns, the Spanish privateer had old and weather-beaten sails and the mainsail had three "remarkably" large patches of new cloth in it. However, the *Santa María* privateer, commanded by Don Martín d' Hamassa, on December 2 took the *Neptune* of Charleston en route to Port Royal which the Spaniards later burnt. On the night of December 4 the *Santa María* landed on North Island where the Spaniards surprised and plundered the pilot's house and took a large new longboat belonging to the *Elizabeth and Mary.* Several English vessels chased by her December 5 and 6 escaped. But on December 7 she took the *Black-Prince,* bound from New York for Charleston; and on December 8 the *Catherine* of St. Croix, bound for Georgia—the latter of which she ordered to Saint Augustine. On December 9 part of the privateer's crew—having missed the privateer—went down the coast in the longboat taken earlier in the week as far as the Raccoon Keys where they went ashore and plundered a plantation—killing some cattle and hogs, and taking three Negroes, two of whom later escaped. The English sent one Issac Maryck to alarm some other plantations on the Santee River (in central South Carolina) and to stop a rice-loaded schooner from coming out of the river. Everyday that week the Spanish privateer was either seen or her signal guns for the longboat heard. She cruised in the same station off the South Carolina coast until

71

December 10 when she permitted the captain of the *Black-Prince* to ransom his pillaged ship for 600 dollars; and also took the *General-Wolfe* off the port of Charleston with a valuable cargo of French prize indigo, sugar, coffee, fruits, and 250 pounds sterling in cash.[136] The plucky Spaniards thus plied the South Carolina coast for over a week, took several vessels, and even raided some settlements; yet eluded capture by both the *Mercury* and the *Epreuve*.

Spanish privateering infested the Southeastern waters until early in 1763. Don Martín and other Spanish privateersmen persisted in preying on the English shipping, and the English in turn sent out vessels in quest of them. On January 19, 1763, the British snow *Epreuve* appeared off the bar at Saint Augustine and retook four English vessels, reportedly taken earlier by the Spaniards off Havana, which were unloading cargoes of fish, pork, wine, flour, soap, and candles.[137] The same month, however, there were at least four privateers out on cruises from Saint Augustine—one to ply the waters off the coasts of New York and Philadelphia, one off South Carolina, and two off Havana, one of the latter being Don Martín's sloop. In addition, two other privateers were preparing to sail from the Florida garrison.[138]

Conditions at Saint Augustine
1762-1763

The stoppage of the trade with her English neighbors compelled the Spaniards at Saint Augustine to turn to privateering to survive. From the summer of 1762 until the following spring, the small Spanish garrison in the Florida colony held out in the face of overwhelming odds. The conditions within the colony were most critical.

In July, 1762, six deserters arrived in Georgia from Saint Augustine and said that more would follow. Hard duty, the lack of pay, and the "want of provisions" in the Spanish garrison forced them "to it." They told of two French privateers being at the Florida outpost earlier in the month and said that a number of Spanish vessels intended to fit out from there as soon as they could get commissions and "provisions," a sloop being expected daily from the northward with some supplies.

72

One of the French vessels and a small Spanish schooner from Cuba had brought to the tiny outpost the news that Havana was under siege which "greatly dispirited that garrison and alarmed the inhabitants."[139] Consequently—after the fall of Havana later that month—the deserters told the Georgians that because Saint Augustine was "much distressed" and her military force not over five hundred men, a very small English force could take the fortress "when they hear the Havanna is taken."[140]

By August, 1762, Saint Augustine was indeed a despairing garrison, the inhabitants having nothing but flour to subsist on. Thus their privateers plied the waters off the English colonies, while the *South-Carolina Gazette* complained late in the summer that never since the beginning of the war were the Southeastern waters so infested with privateers as in the previous six or eight weeks—"whence we may reasonably conclude, that the distressed situation of that garrison has forced them to send out most of those vessels that have lately annoyed our trade, in order to get provisions."[141]

Despite the efforts of her intrepid privateersmen, the conditions in Saint Augustine continued to deteriorate. In the fall of 1762, the garrison was in "greater distress than ever" due to the lack of provisions. The Floridians had not received any supplies from the English colonies since the previous April, except for some rice brought in by one of their privateers in a prize captured early in September off the Carolina coast. The same privateer took two additional English schooners later in September, but the Spaniards unfortunately lost both the prizes and the privateer going into the harbor at Saint Augustine and failed to save any part of the cargoes. Since there was not much left of the rice brought in earlier, the Floridians had to subsist chiefly on fish. Moreover, the garrison did not dare to stir out for a stick of wood "for fear of the Creek Indians" and was "extremely uneasy" and daily apprehensive of a visit from the English. The Spaniards, however, planned to fit out two or three privateers by the beginning of November to ply the Southeastern waters in quest of the provisions so desperately needed.[142]

Early in November, 1762, the *Saint Joseph* privateer of Saint

Augustine captured a schooner bound from New York for Havana with a cargo of beef, pork, wines, etc. which would have been most welcome at the Florida colony. Unfortunately for the nearly starving garrison, the prize became separated from the *Saint Joseph* in a gale. The crew on board the prize knew nothing of navigation and upon meeting two English coasting schooners asked the directions for Saint Augustine. Told by one of the English captains that they should get a pilot if they followed him, the "foolish" and unfortunate Spaniards were led into an English colonial harbor where the British seized the vessel. The Spaniards told their captors, that in addition to the privateer to which they belonged, two other Spanish schooners and a French sloop were out on cruises from Saint Augustine and "that their supplies of every thing depend on the captures to be made by these privateers."[143]

Thus early in December, 1762, the Florida garrison was still in great distress for want of supplies, which explains the daring exploits of Don Martín off the Carolina coast. Fortunately for the Spanish garrison, Don Martín was successful in capturing some supplies. Moreover, the same month a pay sloop got in from Vera Cruz with fifty thousand dollars and two prizes.[144] Two or three other vessels also arrived in Saint Augustine during the winter from Vera Cruz. These ships brought about two hundred barrels of flour and some other provisions without which the garrison would have been in a "starving condition," but even with them it was still in "very great distress." However, they daily expected other vessels from the Mexican port.[145]

These other vessels apparently did not arrive. For in January, 1763, Saint Augustine was yet in such great distress that Don Joseph García upon capturing a vessel with a cargo of rice and pork dispatched it "immediately thither."[146] It was this same month, however, that the *Epreuve,* appeared off Saint Augustine and retook four other prizes whose cargoes were being unloaded for the desperate garrison.

The very existence of the small garrison remained precarious until the end of the war. Compelled by overwhelming necessity to fit out privateers in order to obtain provisions to sustain the garrison, the Spanish colony was barely able to hold its own. Yet the tiny outpost did hold out.

The End of an Era

In the treaty concluded at Paris on February 10, 1763, Great Britain restored Cuba to Spain, and the Spanish crown in turn ceded to Great Britain Florida with fort Saint Augustine, Pensacola, and all that Spain possessed in the North American continent "to the East, or to the South East, of the river Mississippi."[147] Thus Great Britain won Georgia and Florida in Cuba. At Saint Augustine the Spaniards, who had endured such hardships in the closing stages of the war, appeared "dissatisfied at St. Augustine's being given up," and pretended to believe that the colony would not be ceded but that negotiations were under way to allow Great Britain "some advantages in trade, in lieu of it."[148] But Great Britain took possession of Florida on July 21, 1763, thereby ending the long Spanish era (1565-1763).

FOOTNOTES

CHAPTER IV

FLORIDA ENJOYS A THRIVING TRADE WITH HER ENGLISH NEIGHBORS UNTIL THE OUTBREAK OF WAR, 1748-1763

1. *Gazette*, May 20, 1752.
2. *Gazette*, May 18-21, 1750.
3. *Gazette*, October 29 - November 5, 1750.
4. *Ibid.*
5. *Gazette*, May 13-20, 1751.
6. *Gazette*, March 23, 1752.
7. *Gazette*, February 5-12, 1754.
8. *Gazette*, April 26 - May 3, 1760.
9. *Gazette*, May 13-16, 1761.
10. *Gazette*, April 10-17, 1762.
11. *Gazette*, November 12-19, 1750.
12. *Ibid.*
13. *Gazette*, February 2-11, 1751.

14. *Gazette*, August 19-26, 1751.

15. *Gazette*, January 27, 1752.

16. *Gazette*, December 13, 1751.

17. *Gazette*, May 20, 1752.

18. *Gazette*, February 8, May 20, 1752.

19. *Gazette*, February 1, 1752.

20. *Gazette*, May 20, 1752.

21. *Gazette*, January 1, 1753.

22. *Gazette*, January 8, 1753.

23. *Gazette*, April 11, 1753.

24. *Gazette*, December 24, 1753.

25. *Gazette*, February 26 - March 5, 1754.

26. *Gazette*, December 17, 1753.

27. *Gazette*, March 12-19, 1754.

28. *Gazette*, May 15, 1755.

29. *Gazette*, September 18-25, 1755.

30. *Gazette*, September 12-21, 1748.

31. *Gazette*, September 21, October 3-10, October 17-24, October 24-31, November 21 - December 3, December 19-26, 1748.

32. Customs Records, *Gazette*, 1749.

33. Customs Records, *Gazette*, 1750.

34. Customs Records, *Gazette*, 1751-1763; CO/SC, 5: 510, fols. 46-122, Shipping Returns, 1753-1763.

35. Customs Records, *Gazette*, 1756; TePaske, *Governorship of Spanish Florida*, pp. 73-76.

36. Customs Records, *Gazette*, 1749-1763.

37. J. H. Easterby, ed., *The Colonial Records of South Carolina: Journal of the Commons House of Assembly, March 28, 1749 - March 19, 1750* (Columbia, 1962), p. 285. (Hereafter cited as Easterby, *Colonial Records of South Carolina, 1749-1750*.)

38. *Gazette*, September 22-29, 1759.

39. TePaske, *Governorship of Spanish Florida*, pp. 90-91.

40. *Ibid.*, p. 105.

41. TePaske, "Economic Problems," p. 51.

42. TePaske, *Governorship of Spanish Florida*, pp. 72-76.

43. Easterby, *Colonial Records of South Carolina, 1749-1750*, p. xii.

44. *Ibid.*, p. 98.

45. *Ibid.*, p. 100.

46. *Ibid.*, p. 285.

47. *Ibid.*, p. 286.

48. *Ibid.*, p. 285.

49. *Gazette*, September 1, 1752.

50. CO/SC, 5: 510, fol. 46, Shipping Returns, March 26, 1753.

51. CO/NY, 5: 1227, fols. 176, 206, Shipping Returns, October 13, 1753, July 3, 1754.

52. *Gazette*, October 21-28, November 25, 1756; February 10, 1757.

53. Carver J. Harris, ed., "The Memorial of William Walton, of the City of New York, Merchant," *El Escribano*, III (July, 1966), 14-15.

54. *Ibid.*, p. 16.

55. *Ibid.*

56. *Ibid.*

57. *Ibid.*, p. 15.

58. *Ibid.*, pp. 14, 19-21.

59. *Ibid.*, p. 15.

60. *Ibid.*, pp. 14-15.

61. *Ibid.*, p. 16.

62. Ohio Historical Society, Manuscripts Department, Siebert Collection, box 49, fold. 3, typed copy of a letter from W. Sharpe, Secretary to the Treasury, to the Officers of the Customs in the Province of New York, August 11, 1757.

63. *Gazette*, October 21-28, 1756.

64. *Gazette*, November 25, 1756.

65. *Gazette*, February 10, 1757.

66. *Gazette*, April 1, June 30, 1757.

67. *Gazette*, June 23, 1757.

68. *Ibid.*

69. *Gazette*, July 21, 1757.

70. *Ibid.*

71. *Gazette*, August 4, 1757.

72. *Gazette*, October 13, 1757.

73. *Gazette*, August 4-11, 1758.

74. *Gazette*, August 25 - September 1, 1758.

75. *Gazette*, October 20-27, 1758.

76. *Gazette*, December 15-22, 1758.

77. *Gazette*, February 24 - March 3, 1759.

78. Customs Records, *Gazette*, 1759; CO/SC, 5: 510, fols. 66-77, Shipping Returns, 1759.

79. CO/SC, 5: 510, fol. 76, Shipping Returns, May 11, 1759.

80. CO/VA, 5: 1448, fol. 19, Shipping Returns, April 17, 1760.

81. CO/SC, 5: 510, fol. 93, Shipping Returns, September 18, 1760.

82. Allen D. Candler, comp., *The Colonial Records of the State of Georgia* (hereafter cited as Candler, *Colonial Records of Georgia*), Vol. VIII:*Journal of the Proceedings of the Governor and Council, March 8, 1759, to December 31, 1762* (Atlanta, 1907), p. 324.

83. *Ibid.*, p. 347.

84. *Gazette*, August 8-15, 1761.

85. *Gazette*, March 16-20, 1762.

86. Candler, *Colonial Records of Georgia*, VIII, 687.

87. *Ibid.*

88. Library of Congress, Force Transcript, Georgia Proclamations, 1754-1778, Proclamation of Governor James Wright, May 25, 1762, p. 51.

89. Candler, *Colonial Records of Georgia*, VIII, 688-91, 702.

90. *Gazette*, May 29 - June 5, 1762.

91. *Ibid.*

92. *Gazette*, July 17-24, 1762.

93. *Gazette*, September 8-15, October 6-13, 1758.

94. *Gazette*, August 23-30, 1760.

95. *Gazette*, November 25 - December 2, 1756.

96. *Gazette*, August 18, 1757.

97. *Gazette*, June 9, 1757.

98. *Gazette*, June 30 - July 7, 1759.

99. *Gazette*, January 13, 1757.

100. *Gazette*, May 26, 1757.

101. *Gazette*, May 25 - June 2, 1759.

102. William L. Saunders, ed., *The Colonial Records of North Carolina*, Vol. V: *1752-1759* (Raleigh, 1887), pp. 756-57.

103. *Gazette*, June 23, 1757.

104. *Ibid.*

105. *Ibid.*

106. *Gazette*, August 4, 1757.

107. *Gazette*, June 30, 1758.

108. *Gazette*, July 28 - August 4, 1758.

109. *Ibid.*

110. *Gazette*, June 30 - July 7, 1758.

111. *Gazette*, August 25 - September 1, 1758.

112. *Gazette*, October 2-6, 1758.

113. *Gazette*, March 24-31, 1759.

114. *Gazette*, August 8-15, 1761.

115. *Gazette*, March 20-27, April 3-10, April 17-24, 1762.

116. *Gazette*, August 14-21, 1762.

117. *Gazette*, May 15-22, 1762.

118. *Gazette*, April 17-24, 1762.

119. *Gazette*, July 3, 1762.

120. *Gazette*, April 10-17, 1762.

121. *Gazette*, May 22-29, 1762.

122. *Gazette*, April 17-24, 1762.

123. *Gazette*, May 22-29, 1762.

124. *Gazette*, May 15-22, 1762.

125. *Gazette*, July 10-17, 1762.

126. *Gazette*, July 24, 1762.

127. *Gazette*, August 28 - September 4, 1762.

128. *Gazette*, January 29 - February 5, 1763.

129. *Gazette*, August 28 - September 4, 1762.

130. *Gazette*, September 18-25, 1762.

131. *Ibid.*

132. *Gazette*, October 16-23, 1762.

133. *Gazette*, October 23-30, 1762.

134. *Gazette,* September 18-25, November 27 - December 4, 1762; January 22-29, 1763.

135. *Gazette,* December 11, 1762.

136. *Gazette,* December 11, December 18-25, 1762; December 25 - January 1, 1763.

137. *Gazette,* January 29 - February 5, 1763.

138. *Ibid.*

139. *Gazette,* July 17-24, July 24-31, 1762.

140. *Ibid.*

141. *Gazette,* August 21-28, September 11-18, 1762.

142. *Gazette,* October 23-30, 1762.

143. *Gazette,* November 20-27, 1762.

144. *Gazette,* December 18-25, 1762.

145. *Gazette,* January 15-22, 1763.

146. *Gazette,* January 29 - February 5, 1763.

147. *Gazette,* February 5-12, May 21-28, 1763.

148. *Gazette,* April 23-30, May 14, 1763.

CHAPTER V

CONCLUSION: AN APPRAISAL OF FLORIDA'S ECONOMIC PROBLEMS

Spanish Florida enjoyed a thriving—although clandestine—commerce with her English neighbors in the mid-eighteenth century (1732-1763). Strategically located to protect the Spanish fleets sailing through the Bahama Channel and to prevent foreign encroachment of Mexico, the Gulf Coast, and the Southeast, the Florida colony, nevertheless, to supply its everyday wants turned to the encroaching English colonies. Moreover, the English colonies—eager to take advantage of any opportunity to trade with Spanish America—provided the Spaniards in the tiny outpost at Saint Augustine with much-needed supplies in spite of England's efforts to squeeze Spain out of the Southeast.

A poor, neglected, and unpopular outpost of the Spanish Empire in America, Saint Augustine turned to the nearby English colonies despite Spain's stringent trade restrictions. The unreliability of the Florida *situado* or of any aid from Spain or Spanish-American sources virtually compelled the Floridians to look elsewhere. In fact, at times the Spanish crown itself allowed the illicit traffic. After 1750 the Havana Company had permission to purchase supplies in the English colonies if no supplies could be secured elsewhere for the garrison at Saint Augustine. Whether this was the result of a sense of guilt over the colony's neglect or only expediency is uncertain. In any event, the Floridians usually welcomed the English goods, especially in times of scarcity or want.

Yet Spanish Florida was not a totally helpless, unproductive frontier outpost. Early in the eighteenth century the Floridians imported supplies from the neighboring English colonies. Cattle, "porke," "Pease," corn, rum, dry goods, and "Iron Potts" all arrived at Saint Augustine from the neighboring English colonies. But, in turn, the Floridians sent the English colonies not only gold and silver, but oftentimes the produce of their own colony—oranges, fish and sea tortoises, and deerskins, for example. The unreliability of the *situado* or of any aid from Spain or the nearby Spanish colonies also spurred the Spaniards in the Southeast to develop any potentially productive enterprises within the colony. Oranges, for example, grew in abundance, thus giving rise to Florida's infant orange industry which was a welcome supplement to and at times a substitute for the *situado* prior to the War of Jenkins' Ear. Consequently, English traders stopping at Saint Augustine not only found a warm welcome for their goods, but frequently found produce to take back to the English colonies.

During the War of Jenkins' Ear and the French and Indian War, privateering was the supplement or substitute for the *situado*. Both wars interrupted most, if not all, of the trade between the English and the Spanish in the Southeast. But the intrepid Spanish privateersmen took over the task of supplying the tiny Florida outpost. Privateers from Saint Augustine plied the waters off the nearby English colonies—spurred on by their colony's plight. Eluding capture, they succeeded in annoying their English neighbors; but more importantly, they were successful in supplying the small Spanish colony with much-needed goods.

Tied economically to the English colonies by the mid-eighteenth century, Spanish Florida was no longer solely dependent economically upon the *situado* or other aid from Spain or her colonies. Free trade with the English colonies, as Montiano realized, was a solution to the major economic problems of the Florida colony—especially since the colony was not without its own productive enterprises. In effect, free trade existed—except in time of war. In fact, trade between the Spanish and the English in the Southeast became common practice partly because it provided more satisfactorily for Saint Augustine's needs than the monopolistic Spanish commercial system designed primarily for the benefit of Spain, but often stifling for her colonies; and partly because the traffic apparently added to the economic development and prosperity of the English colonies too—the English were not just being neighborly. On the contrary, it helped fill the pocketbooks of merchants like William Walton and Samuel Piles, but at the same time boosted the economy of, for example, South Carolina.

In times of peace, both the English and the Spanish in the Southeast winked at all trade restrictions. In times of war, the intrepid Spanish privateers supplied the Saint Augustine garrison with the much-needed English goods. In effect, the English colonies, willingly or unwillingly, helped their Spanish neighbor to hold out in the Southeast.

APPENDIX I

MANIFESTS OF CARGOES RELATING TO TRADE BETWEEN CHARLESTON AND SAINT AUGUSTINE (1716-1763)

Date of Entry or Exit	Vessels Name	Masters Name	Cargo	Whence From or Where Bound
January 28 1716	Sloop *Industry* of Carolina	John Watson	Onle ballast	From Saint Augustine
February 14 1716	Sloop *Fortune* of Carolina	Peter Bouge	30 Barrils Porke 20 do Beefe 5 Cagg rum 4 Barrills salt 6 Barrills Flower 1 do Hering 40 cheeses European Goods p. certif	Bound to Saint Augustine
February 20 1716	Sloop *Mary* of Carolina	James Banbery	38 Barrills Beef & Pork 28 do Flower 7 Barrills Rum & Caggs Brandy 26 Furkins butter 5 casks Salt 10 caggs of Rum European goods p. certifica being goods returned not sold	From Saint Augustine
August 1716	Sloop *Industry* of South Carolina	George Smith	31 barrills beefe & porke a pcll butter & cheese 613 gall rum 42 gall sperritts 49 barrills flower European goods per certifica being all goods returned unsold	From Saint Augustine
January 6 1717	Sloop *Industry* of Carolina	Joseph Palmer	Ballast Only	From Saint Augustine
January 11 1717	Shallop *Golden Fleece* of Carolina	Jonathon Tubb	15 Barrls Beefe 35 Casks of Flower 11 Barrills of Rum & European goods p. certifica Exported hence in ye sloop and returned	From Saint Augustine
January 11 1717	Sloop *Turtle* of Carolina	Richard Wood	4 Hhd 1 terce of Rum 83 barrils Beefe & Pork 6 barrills of Flower. European goods p. certifica	Bound to Saint Augustine
January 11 1717	Sloop *Mary* of Carolina	James Banbery	38 Barrills beefe & Porke 52 Barrils Flower 7 barrills 17 Caggs Rum 8 Caggs of Sperritts a (and) European goods p. certifica	Bound to Saint Augustine

Date of Entry or Exit	Vessels Name	Masters Name	Cargo	Whence From or Where Bound
January 15 1717	Sloop *Katherine* of Carolina	John Watson	Ballast only	From Saint Augustine
April 3 1717	Sloop *Industry* of Carolina	Richard Dwelly	31 Barrills Beefe & Pork a pcl. Butter & cheese 616 gall Rum 42 Gall sperritts 29 Barrills Flower European goods p. cert.	Bound to Saint Augustine
December 11 1717	Sloop *Industry* of Carolina	Joseph Palmer	4 Barrills Porke 9 Cask & pipes Tryall wine 1 Cask sperritts 3 terces 13 Barrills 4 Caggs Rum a pcll Bolled Rum 19 Barrills Beef 64 Cask Flower a pcll of Cheese 4 Cask Bread European Goods p. certifica	Bound to Saint Augustine
December 25 1717	Sloop *Swan and Eagle* of Carolina	John Dolton	Only Oringes (Oranges)	From Saint Augustine
April 14 1718	Schooner *Brothers* of Carolina	Richard Norcomb	Only Ballast	From Saint Augustine
April 18 1718	Sloop *Katherine* of Carolina	John Watson	200 bls Flower 4 Hhds 8 lbs Rum 13 bls spirits 3 casks Canary a parcll cheese 1 cask bacon a Bll Salt Dry goods as p. cert.	Bound to Saint Augustine
May 16 1718	Schooner *Brothers* of Carolina	Richard Norcomb	16 Cask Rum 5 bls Flower 1 bll Beef a parcll of cheese European goods as p. certificate All returned	From Saint Augustine
August 16 1718	Brig. *Saint Augustine*	Richard Fifield	15 Blls Red Herrings 1 Box Merchandize 2 casks of Knives 2 peices (pieces) cotton	Bound to Saint Augustine
November 1 1718	Schooner *Margarett* of Carolina	Joseph Palmer	1 Cask 4 boxes dry goods 4 Caggs wine 26 Blls 4 Caggs 6 Cases Spirits 88 Cheese	Bound to Saint Augustine
	Schooner *Margarett* of Carolina	Joseph Palmer	Only Ballast	From Saint Augustine
March 31 1731	Sloop *Prince Frederick* of South Carolina	John Cowley	Ballast	From Saint Augustine
May 17 1731	Schooner *Good Hope* of South Carolina	John Frazier	Ballast only	From Saint Augustine

Date of Entry or Exit	Vessels Name	Masters Name	Cargo	Whence From or Where Bound
June 14 1731	Sloop *Prince Frederick* of South Carolina	John Cowley	Parcell of Oranges	From Saint Augustine
October or November 21 1731	Schooner *Good Hope* of South Carolina	Samuel Parsons	Ballast Only	Bound to Saint Augustine
May 13 1732	Schooner *Good Hope* of South Carolina	Samuel Parsons	Parcell of fruit	From Saint Augustine
January 21 1732	*King William* of London		Parcel of fruit	From Saint Augustine
January 31 1733	Sloop *Orange* of Providence	Benjamin Austin	Parcell of fruit	From Saint Augustine
January 21 1734	Sloop *Virgins Adventure* of Port Royal	James Pollard	Ballast only	From Saint Augustine
February 10 1734	Sloop *Catherine* of Jamaica	Benjamin Munroe	Hhd fish pcell oranges	From Saint Augustine
March 17 1734	Sloop *Endeavour* of Rhode Island	Richard Waterman	Ballast only	From Saint Augustine
April 18 1734	Sloop *Virgins Adventure* of Port Royal	James Pollard	Ballast only	From Saint Augustine
June 10 1734	Sloop *Virgins Adventure* of Port Royal	John Martyn	Ballast only	From Saint Augustine
June 20 1734	Sloop *Elizabeth* of Providence	Benjamin Munroe	Parcell fruit	From Saint Augustine
July 18 1734	Sloop *Virgins Adventure* of Port Royal	John Martyn	Ballast only	From Saint Augustine
January 20 1735	Sloop *Elizabeth* of Providence	Benjamin Munroe	Parcells fruit	From Saint Augustine
February 10 1735	Sloop *Catherine* of Jamaice (Jamaica)	James Crawford	1 hogshead fish parcell oranges	From Saint Augustine
March 17 1735	Sloop *Endeavour* of Rhode Island	Richard Waterman	Ballast only	From Saint Augustine
March 31 1735	Sloop *Katherine (Catherine)* of Jamaica	James Crawford	1 pair old organs Ballast	From Saint Augustine
April 28 1735	Sloop *Elizabeth* of Providence	Benjamin Munro (Munroe)	Ballast only	From Saint Augustine

Date of Entry or Exit	Vessels Name	Masters Name	Cargo	Whence From or Where Bound
May 12 1735	Sloop *Catherine* of Jamaica	James Crawford	Ballast only	From Saint Augustine
July 7 1735	Sloop *Elizabeth* of Providence	Benjamin Munroe	General Cargo 15 Bars Sugar 3 Hhd Rum 44 Baggs & 7 cases & Boxes Sugar 98 Skins 2 Bundles wearing Apparrel Pl empty bottles & 1 Barl Provisions Retd.	From Saint Augustine
July 7 1735	Schooner *Neptune* of Charlestown	Mansfield Tucker	A parcell oringes (oranges)	From Saint Augustine
July 15 or 16 1735	Sloop *True Friends* of Barbados	Samuel Warner	63 loaves Spanish Sugar	From Saint Augustine
September 4 1735	Schooner *Neptune* of Charlestown	Mansfield Tucker	A parcell oringes (oranges)	From Saint Augustine
October 17 1735	Sloop *Ranger* of Charleston	William Gibson	A Parcell of Fruit	From Saint Augustine
October 21 1735	Sloop *True Friends* of Barbadoes	Samuel Warner	28000 Oranges 1 pr glass sconces 7 Bars salt 1 do flower 2 ca fruit 1 pr scales & waits 1 beam & chain	From Saint Augustine
November 8 1735	Schooner *Neptune* of Charleston		A parcell orranges	From Saint Augustine
November 20 1735	Brig. *Edward and Elizabeth* of Charleston	Samuel Parsons	A parcell Orranges	From Saint Augustine
December 10 1735	Sloop *Ranger* of Charleston	William Gibson	800 orranges	From Saint Augustine
December 20 1735	Brig. *Edward and Elizabeth* of Charleston	Samuel Parsons	General Cargo Beef 40 Barls Corn 20 Barls Peas 45 Barls 2 Pipes wine 29 Casks do 2 Hhd Vinegar 2 bars do 4 bars nails 4 Bus dry goods 3 Hhd do all legally imported 10 casks Tallow 30 Casks butter	Bound to Saint Augustine
January 16 1736	Schooner *Neptune* of South Carolina	Mansfield Tucker	Ballast only	From Saint Augustine
February 3 1736	*Edward and Elizabeth* of South Carolina	Edward Parsons	1000 oranges	From Saint Augustine

Date of Entry or Exit	Vessels Name	Masters Name	Cargo	Whence From or Where Bound
February 24 1736	Sloop *Ranger* of South Carolina	William Gibson	A pcell of oranges	From Saint Augustine
March 2 1736	Sloop *Unity* of South Carolina	Henry Bryixe	60 blls flower, 10 firkins butter, 4 blls tallow 2 hhd rum,3 pipes wine & sundry European goods Corn 300 bushells Peas 146 bushells	Bound to Saint Augustine
April 3 1736	Sloop *Rebecah and Mary* of South Carolina	William Watson	4 Blls nails 2 doz hoes & 2 doz axes returned	From Saint Augustine
April 21 1736	Sloop *Unity* of South Carolina	Henry Bryxe	Ballast only	From Saint Augustine
April 22 1736	Brig. *Edward and Elizabeth* of South Carolina	Samuel Parsons	Ballast only	From Saint Augustine
May 21 1736	Sloop *Ranger* of South Carolina	William Gibson	23 chests Spanish sugr contg about 450 ℔ each	From Saint Augustine
May 22 1736	Schooner *Neptune* of South Carolina	Mansfield Tucker	Ballast only	From Saint Augustine
September 2 1736	Sloop *Charming Betty* of Charlestown	Thomas Crostwaite	Ballast only	From Saint Augustine
September 2 1736	Brig. *Edward and Elizabeth* of Charleston	Samuel Parsons	1 bagg cocoa 17700 oranges 2 hhd salt rd (returned)	From Saint Augustine
September 2 1736	Sloop *Rebecca and Mary* of Charleston	William Watson	Abt 500 oranges 5 or 6 deer skins & a pcell of small glasses returned	From Saint Augustine
January 25 1737	Schooner *Neptune* of Charleston	Mansfield Tucker	172 bls flour 3 bls tallow 8 ℔ apples 10 firkins hogs lard 1 pipe & 1 cask wine 7 negroes & 4000 feet pine boards	Bound to Saint Augustine
May 26 1738	Sloop *Charming Betty* of Charleston	Thomas Crosthwaite	Ballast only	From Saint Augustine
June 16 1739	Sloop *Charming Betty* of Charleston	Thomas Crosthwaite	Ballast only	From Saint Augustine
1739	Sloop *Charming Betty* of Charleston	Thomas Crostwait	30 skins of cocoa (and) ballast	From Saint Augustine

THERE IS A GAP IN THE RECORDS FROM 1739-1752

Date of Entry or Exit	Vessels Name	Masters Name	Cargo	Whence From or Where Bound
March 26 1753	*Elizabeth*	Charles Reid	4 Barrl flour 60 Dozn bottled beer 12 barrl Bread 20 Kegs butter 30 grindstones 4 casks beeswax 5 Lb cheese 48 Axes	Bound to Saint Augustine
March 19 1759	*Cornelian*	Jonathan Lawrence	Ballast only	From Saint Augustine
May 11 1759	*Scriven*	Thomas Tucker	Sundry goods per certificate	Bound to Saint Augustine
June 1 1759	*Scriven*	Thomas Tucker	Ballast only	From Saint Augustine
September 1 1759	*Bettsie*	Fryan Foskey	No goods	Bound to Saint Augustine
April 18 1760	*Lark*	Jonathan Lawrence	Ballast only	From Saint Augustine
May 17 1760	*Wolf*	Issac Lawrence	Ballast only	From Saint Augustine
September 18 1760	*Speedwell*	William Rogers	Sundry Brittish goods legally imported	Bound to Saint Augustine
July 21 1763	*Hibernia*	John Butler	Ballast only	From Saint Augustine
July 23 1763	*Endeavour*	Alexander Malcolm	66 casks 2 hampers of rum beer & wine & sundry Britts goods	Bound to Saint Augustine

MANIFESTS OF CARGOES RELATING TO TRADE
BETWEEN NEW YORK AND SAINT AUGUSTINE
(1732-1755)

Date of Entry or Exit	Vessels Name	Masters Name	Cargo	Whence From or Where Bound
May 24 1732	*Mary* of New York	Abraham Kip for Jacob Kip	Ballast	From Saint Augustine
August 2 1732	*Swallow* of New York	William Joggets	Ballast	From Saint Augustine
October 9 1732	*Mary* of New York	Abraham Kip	Ballast	From Saint Augustine
March 23 1733	*°Jaccob* of New York	Abraham Kip	Ballast	From Saint Augustine
June 25 1733	*Jaccob* of New York	Abraham Kip	Ballast	From Saint Augustine
November 28 1733	*Jaccob* of New York	Abraham Kip	Ballast	From Saint Augustine
April 29 1734	*Jaccob* of New York	Abraham Kip	Ballast	From Saint Augustine
December 12 1734	*Jaccob* of New York	Abraham Kip	Ballast	From Saint Augustine
April 3 1735	*Jaccob* of New York	Abraham Kip	Ballast	From Saint Augustine
June 2 1735	*Neptune* of South Carolina	Mansfield Tucker	Ballast	From Saint Augustine
November 7 1735	*Jacob* (Jaccob) of New York	Abraham Kip	Ballast	From Saint Augustine
April 19 1736	*Jacob* of New York	Abraham Kip	Ballast	From Saint Augustine
April 2 1737	*°Don Carlos* of New York	Abraham Kip	Ballast	From Saint Augustine
July 23 1737	*Don Carlos* of New York	Abraham Kip	Ballast	From Saint Augustine
October 13 1737	*Don Carlos* of New York	Abraham Kip	9 Negroes	From Saint Augustine
January 1 1738	*Don Carlos* of New York	Abraham Kip	Ballast	From Saint Augustine
March 24 1738	*Don Carlos* of New York	Abraham Kip	1 box Succads	From Saint Augustine
April 26 1738	*Jacob* of New York	David Griffith	Ballast	From Saint Augustine
July 3 1738	*Don Carlos* of New York	Abraham Kip	Ballast	From Saint Augustine
July 18 1738	*Jacob* of New York	David Griffith	Ballast	From Saint Augustine

Date of Entry or Exit	Vessels Name	Masters Name	Cargo	Whence From or Where Bound
September 6 1738	*Don Carlos* of New York	Abraham Kip	Ballast	From Saint Augustine
October 16 1738	*Jacob* of New York	David Griffith	Ballast	From Saint Augustine
October 31 1738	*Dom Phillip* of New York	Lewis Thibon	3 casks oranges	From Saint Augustine
March 9 1739	*Jacob* of New York	David Griffith	Ballast	From Saint Augustine
April 9 1739	*Jacob* of New York	David Griffiths (Griffith)	Ballast	From Saint Augustine
June 18 1739	*Jacob* of New York	David Griffith	Ballast	From Saint Augustine
July 16 1739	*Don Carlos* of New York	Abraham Kip	Ballast	From Saint Augustine
July 25 1739	*Don Carlos* of New York	Abraham Kip	Ballast	From Saint Augustine
November 2 1739	*Don Carlos* of New York	Abraham Kip	Ballast	From Saint Augustine
November 3 1739	*Jacob* of New York	David Griffith	Ballast	From Saint Augustine
November 6 1739	*Jacob* of New York	David Griffith	Ballast	From Saint Augustine
October 13 1753	*St. Augustin* of New York	Richard Wright	Package The package & contents of other goods 10,000 ft plank	From Saint Augustine
July 3 1754	*Lark* of New York	William Hyer	17 sea tortoises	From Saint Augustine
September 13 1754	*Lena* of New York	Jonathon Lawrence	41 packs deerskins 17 tons logwood	Bound to Saint Augustine
May 9 1755	*St. Augustine* (St. Augustin) of New York		31 packs deerskins 9 aroons of Coxtex ceriuranus (sic)	Bound to Saint Augustine
October 6 1755	*Lark* of New York	William Hyer	60 tons provis for landing only there conformable to Act of Assembly 10 casks Mada wine, 6 casks rum, British plantn produce on oath Europ. goods on Corgte 2 horses	Bound to Saint Augustine

°William Walton (senior and junior) owned two of the above ships—probably the *Jaccob* (*Jacob*) and the *Don Carlos*.

APPENDIX III

MANIFESTS OF CARGOES RELATING TO TRADE BETWEEN VIRGINIA AND SAINT AUGUSTINE

(1759-1760)

Date of Entry or Exit	Vessels Name	Masters Name	Cargo	Whence From or Where Bound
November 25 1759	Sloop *Cornelia*	John Lawrence	6 boxes forn sugar Rum 1 hhd	From Saint Augustine
April 17 1760	Sloop *Cornelia*	John Lawrence	4 blls lard 6 Tos Beef 100 bus salt 53 Iron Potts Pork Blls 300 Flour Blls 160 Staves & Shingles 3000	Bound to Saint Augustine

APPENDIX IV

MANIFESTS OF CARGOES RELATING TO TRADE BETWEEN GEORGIA AND SAINT AUGUSTINE

(1760)

Date of Entry or Exit	Vessels Name	Masters Name	Cargo	Whence From or Where Bound
December 17 1760	Schooner *Elizabeth*	Thomas Cox	Ballast	From Saint Augustine
December 22 1760	Schooner *Elizabeth*	Thomas Cox		Bound to Saint Augustine

NOTE: Except for words in parentheses, the items listed under the heading Cargo are in the form in which I received them.

Hhd - hogshead
ca - cask
bars - barrels

BIBLIOGRAPHY OF WORKS CITED

(I. MANUSCRIPTS)

Great Britain. Public Record Office MSS. Colonial Office.
1. Georgia, Shipping Returns, Class Five. Number 709.
2. New York, Shipping Returns, Class Five. Numbers 1225-1228.
3. South Carolina, Shipping Returns, Class Five. Numbers 508-510.
4. Virginia, Shipping Returns, Class Five. Numbers 1444-1449.
Ohio Historical Society. Manuscripts Department, Siebert Collection. Typed copies.
U. S. Library of Congress. East Florida Papers, Letters to the Captain General (Montiano Letters), 1737-1741. Copies.
U. S. Library of Congress. Force Transcript, Georgia Proclamations, 1754-1778.

(II. PUBLISHED DOCUMENTS AND LAWS)

Candler, Allen D., ed. *The Colonial Records of the State of Georgia.* 24 vols. Atlanta, 1904-1915.
Carroll, B. R., comp. *Historical Collections of South Carolina: Embracing Many Rare and Valuable Pamphlets and Other Documents Relating to the History of the State from its Discovery to its Independence.* 2 vols. New York, 1836.
Collections of the Georgia Historical Society, Vol. VII, Pt. I. "Letters of Montiano, Siege of Saint Augustine." Savannah, 1909.
Davenport, Frances Gardiner, ed. *European Treaties Bearing on the History of the United States and its Dependencies.* 4 vols. Washington, D.C., 1917, 1929, 1934, 1937.
Easterby, J. H., ed. *The Colonial Records of South Carolina: Journal of the Commons House of Assembly.* 9 vols. Columbia, 1951-1962.
Saunders, William L., ed. *The Colonial Records of North Carolina.* 30 vols. Raleigh, 1886-1890.
Towle, Dorothy S., ed. *Records of the Vice-Admiralty Court of Rhode Island, 1716-1752.* American Legal Records, Vol. III. Washington, D.C., 1936.

(III. BOOKS)

Bolton, Herbert E. *The Spanish Borderlands, A Chronicle of Old Florida and the Southwest.* New Haven, 1921.
Chatelain, Verne E. *The Defenses of Spanish Florida, 1565 to 1763.* Washington, D.C., 1941.
Fernández-Flórez, Dario. *The Spanish Heritage in the United States.* Madrid, 1965.
Forbes, James Grant. *Sketches, Historical and Topographical, of the Floridas: More Particularly of East Florida.* Gainesville, 1964.

Haring, Clarence H. *The Spanish Empire in America*. New York, 1947, and New York, 1963.

Jameson, John Franklin, ed. *Privateering and Piracy in the Colonial Period: Illustrative Documents*. New York, 1923.

Lanning, John Tate. *The Diplomatic History of Georgia: A Study of the Epoch of Jenkins' Ear*. Chapel Hill, 1936.

Romans, Bernard. *A Concise Natural History of East and West Florida*. Gainesville, 1962.

TePaske, John Jay. *The Governorship of Spanish Florida, 1700-1763*. Durham, 1964.

(IV. AUTHORITIES: PERIODICALS)

Arnade, Charles W. "Cattle Raising in Spanish Florida." *Agricultural History*, XXXV (July, 1961), 116-24.

Chatelain, Verne E. "Spanish Contributions in Florida to American Culture." *Florida Historical Quarterly*, XIX (January, 1941), 213-44.

Harris, J. Carver, ed. "The Memorial of William Walton, of the City of New York, Merchant." *El Escribano*, III (July, 1966), 14-22.

Lawson, Edward W. "What Became of the Man Who Cut Off Jenkins' Ear?" *Florida Historical Quarterly*, XXXVII (July, 1958 - April, 1959), 33-41.

Norton, B., ed. "Journal of a Privateersman." *Atlantic Monthly*, July-December, 1861, pp. 353-59, 417-24.

Robinson, T. Ralph. "Some Aspects of the History of Citrus in Florida." *Quarterly Journal of the Florida Academy of Sciences*, VIII (March, 1945), 59-66.

TePaske, John Jay. "Economic Problems of the Florida Governors." *Florida Historical Quarterly*, XXXVI (September, 1958), 42-52.

(V. NEWSPAPERS)

South-Carolina Gazette (Charleston), 1732-1763.

South Carolina Weekly Gazette (Charleston), 1758-1759.

INDEX

Moro Castle, 69
Munroe (Munro), Benjamin, 15, 85-86

Nails, 16, 86-87
Naval Stores, 70
Negroes, 8, 17, 41, 67, 70-71, 87, 89; British South Sea Company obtains *asiento* to import and sell in Spanish-America, 6; desert from Saint Augustine, 37; Florida governor promises Georgia to restore runaway, 60
Neptune (vessel), 15, 17, 71, 86-87, 89
Newcastle, Duke of, 7
New York: illicit trade with Saint Augustine, 5, 12-14, 16, 21-23, 52-57, 59, 89; illicit trade with Spanish-American colonies, 5; merchant cites advantages of trade with Saint Augustine, 56-57; privateer of, 65; Saint Augustine sends privateer to ply coast of, 72
Norcomb, Richard, 84
North Carolina, 1, 11; privateers, 35-36
North Island, 71
Nova Scotia, 65

Occoni Indians, 58
Ogeachy, 58
Oglethorpe, James, 9, 29, 33, 35, 38
Orange (vessel), 14, 85
Oranges: Florida exports to English colonies, 14-16, 21-24, 81, 84-87, 90; Georgia exports juice of, 24; grow easily in area around Saint Augustine, 23; infant industry at Saint Augustine, 22-24; introduction of into New World, 23; South Carolina grows and exports, 24
Orange Juice, 24
Organs, 85

Palacio y Valenzuela, Lucas Fernando de, 60
Palacre James (vessel), 70
Palmer, Joseph, 83-84
Paris, 75
Parliament, 25, 27, 62
Parris, John, 10
Parsons, Edward, 86
Parsons, Samuel, 14-15, 85-87
Patiño, Joseph, 10
Peas, 16, 23, 61, 80, 86-87
Peggy (vessel), 65
Pensacola, 61, 75
Phenix (vessel), 35
Philadelphia, 23, 72
Philip V, 25-28, 47-50. *See also*

Spain
Piles, Samuel, 61-62, 82
Pine Boards, 17, 87
Pitch, 36
Plank, 55, 90
Plate, 8. *See also* Gold; Silver; Money
Political State, 25
Pollard, James, 15, 85
Pork, 54, 72, 74, 80, 83-84, 91
Port-au-Prince, 64
Portobello, 6
Porto-Purco, 47
Port Royal (South Carolina), 15, 19, 66
Port Royal (vessel), 14
Portugal, 48
Poultry, 41
Prew, Captain (English captain held prisoner at Havana), 11
Prince Frederick (vessel), 14, 84-85
Prisoners, 34, 36, 40-41, 43
Privateering, 1, 8, 25-28; Florida governor promises to stop aiding French, 60; French and Indian War stimulates, 59-60, 63-74; Georgia attempts to prevent Saint Augustine from aiding French, 59; legalize profession of, 34; outlaw practice of, 34; Saint Augustine active in, 35-40, 59, 63-74; Saint Augustine aids French, 59, 63-68, 71; Saint Augustine depends on, 37-40, 70-74, 82; substitute for *situado*, 81; War of Jenkins' Ear stimulates, 33-40, 42-43. *See also* Trade
Produce, 5-6, 13, 15
Promise of "kind entertainment," 5, 47
Providence (Rhode Island), 14-15, 36, 41-42
Puerto Rico, 5, 7

Raccoon Keys, 71
Ranger (vessel), 86-87
Rebeccah and Mary (vessel), 16, 87
Reid, Charles, 55, 88
Rhode Island, 14-15, 21, 70-71
Rice, 19, 36, 39, 42, 54, 70-72, 74
Río de la Plata, 48
Rogers, William, 59, 88
Roscas (ring-shaped biscuits or cakes), 39
Rose (vessel), 20, 39
Rowse, John, 34-35, 37
Rum, 7, 64, 80, 83-84, 86-88, 90-91. *See also* Beer; Brandy; Wine

Sails, 7-8
Saint Augustine, 8-11; aids French privateers during French and In-